Bridge:
A Thinker's Game

How You Think is More Important than What
and
Thinking Comes Before Doing

Joe Blatnick

authorHOUSE®

AuthorHouse™ LLC
1663 Liberty Drive
Bloomington, IN 47403
www.authorhouse.com
Phone: 1-800-839-8640

Published by AuthorHouse   10/22/2013

ISBN: 978-1-4918-0791-0 (sc)
ISBN: 978-1-4918-0792-7 (e)

Library of Congress Control Number: 2013914849

Any people depicted in stock imagery provided by Thinkstock are models, and such
images are being used for illustrative purposes only.
Certain stock imagery © Thinkstock.

This book is printed on acid-free paper.

Because of the dynamic nature of the Internet, any web addresses or links
contained in this book may have changed since publication and may no longer be
valid. The views expressed in this work are solely those of the author and do not
necessarily reflect the views of the publisher, and the publisher hereby disclaims any
responsibility for them.

Cover and Interior Design and Layout by
Katherine Widziak, www.widziak.com

Caricatures Drawn by
José Bigith

INTRODUCTION

Although true mastery of the game can never be achieved – the combination of hands which can be dealt is a mind-boggling number – playing competently can. When we all embarked on the long journey, our mentors were constantly bombarding us with clichés or myths, if you prefer, which initially helped us begin the learning process but as the learning progressed, we began to realize that these myths were just guidelines. We eventually began to realize that these guidelines had exceptions and that nothing replaced thinking. Here is just a partial list of these myths:

1. Second Hand Low
2. Third Hand High
3. Cover an Honour
4. Split Your Honours
5. Return Partner's Suit
6. Never Under Lead Kings

What really counts is what you learn after you think you know it all.

The list goes on. One of the many negatives which result from this blind obedience to the clichés of yesteryear is the absence of thinking. The newer players think only of the present trick. Those who are a little more experienced will be thinking 2 or 3 tricks ahead while the truly good players are projecting those thoughts well into the play of the hand and in many cases to the 13th trick. It is this ability, as Declarer or as a defender, to plan and look ahead that separates the good from the mediocre players.

Each of the hands which appear in this book, either dispel a myth, reinforce a guideline or show that even good guidelines have exceptions. Whichever of these is the case, one thing will be abundantly clear – thinking wins the day.

Here is a philosophy that applies to life in general. But it could also be applied successfully at the Bridge table.

There are three kinds of people:

~ The "wills" who can accomplish everything.
~ The "won'ts" who criticize everything.
~ The "can'ts" who fail at everything.

BE A 'WILL'

"Quit talking and let's play Bridge."

DEDICATION

*This book is dedicated to all those bridge players out there
who love this game as much as I do.*

ACKNOWLEDGEMENTS

I wish to thank all those bridge players who have bought my other books. Hopefully, you've enjoyed reading them as much as I've enjoyed writing them.

ABOUT THE AUTHOR

Joe should be slowing down but the urge to put on paper, what is in his head, is too much to ignore. Had he become so totally engrossed at an earlier age who knows where it might have led.

TABLE OF CONTENTS

MYTHS

An Old Traditional Story or Legend Giving Expression to Early Beliefs

> *Although bridge is replete with Myths and Guidelines, bridge players must still exercise good judgement and common sense in many situations where simply following these myths dogmatically will lead to failure.*

1) GET THE KIDDIES OFF THE STREET

This statement is simply a colloquial way of saying that you should draw the opponents trump as quickly as possible. The logic behind this advice is that you don't want your winners in the side suits to be trumped. It is very disheartening to have a side suit winner trumped and in many such cases Declarer has only to look in a mirror to know where the fault lies. However, there are exceptions to this advice as there are in almost all of Bridge's *'Rules'*. Basically, Declarer should take the defenders' trump quickly unless one or more of the following conditions exist.

1. Declarer needs to ruff some losers in dummy.
2. Declarer cannot afford to give up the lead.
3. Dummy's trump are needed as entries.
4. Declarer might need to establish a side suit first.

The following hands will illustrate these exceptions.

Ruffing In Dummy

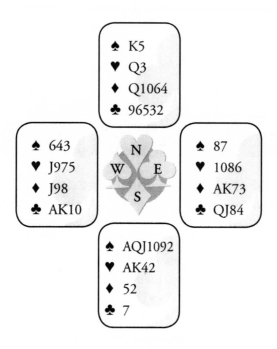

Contract: 4♠   Opening Lead: ♣A

Most players were taught to count losers in a suit contract and winners when playing N.T. If, in a suit contract, they had too many losers their next order of business was to look for a way to eliminate them. However, Declarer must carry this thinking a little further and realize why some cards are not losers. Look at the Hearts in this hand. Declarer's fourth Heart is not considered a loser because it can be trumped in dummy. Yet, how will that happen if the trump are drawn first. Therefore, a Heart must be trumped in dummy before Declarer draws trump. Declarer's winners will then be the six trump in hand, a Heart ruff in dummy and those 3 top Hearts – 10 in all.

Entries

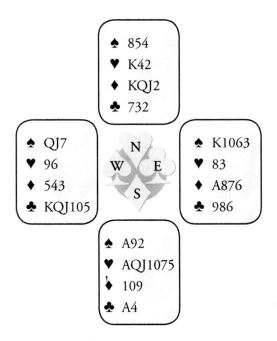

| | ♠ 854 |
| ♥ K42 |
| ♦ KQJ2 |
| ♣ 732 |

♠ QJ7		♠ K1063
♥ 96		♥ 83
♦ 543		♦ A876
♣ KQJ105		♣ 986

| ♠ A92 |
| ♥ AQJ1075 |
| ♦ 109 |
| ♣ A4 |

Contract: 4♥   Opening Lead: ♠K

It would appear that there are four losers – two ♠s, one ♦ and one ♣. However, there are extra winners in Diamonds on which Declarer could discard two losers. But there are a couple of inherent problems in this kind of hand. If Declarer were to try and establish those extra Diamond winners before drawing trump, one of those Diamonds might get ruffed.

And if Declarer were to draw trump first, he might not have an entry to dummy by which to enjoy those Diamonds. The solution is to draw just two rounds of trump, leaving the King in dummy. They might split 2/2 and if they don't, leave the third one out there...that King would then simultaneously draw the defender's last trump and serve as the entry to dummy after the Diamonds were established. So the correct sequence of plays is to win the opening lead, draw two rounds of trump with the Ace and Queen and then lead Diamonds. As luck would have it the two rounds of trump clear the suit

"Let's bid that hand again."

but having played it in the suggested manner is really taking out some insurance. A third round of trump to the King when defenders are out of them is of no consequence. And if one defender shows out on the first trump lead then the Diamond plays must be tried before extracting all defenders' trump.

Losing The Lead

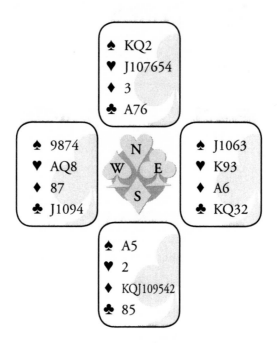

Contract: 5♦   Opening Lead: ♣J

Counting losers reveals one trump, one ♥ and one ♣. If Declarer were to attempt taking away the defenders' trump, those 3 losers would be quick in materializing. That being the case, Declarer must discard one of those losers quickly and as luck would have it, there is an extra Spade winner coming to the rescue. By playing three rounds of Spades and discarding a Club or Heart loser, Declarer is then safe to attack the trump. As can be seen, three rounds of Spades can be cashed without a defender trumping in. Even the more normal 5 – 3 break would not present a problem.

Side Suit

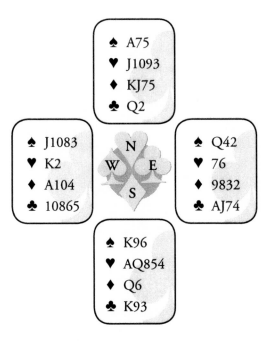

♠ A75
♥ J1093
♦ KJ75
♣ Q2

♠ J1083
♥ K2
♦ A104
♣ 10865

♠ Q42
♥ 76
♦ 9832
♣ AJ74

♠ K96
♥ AQ854
♦ Q6
♣ K93

Contract: 4♥   Opening Lead: ♠J

This hand has a loser in each suit – one too many. The careless Declarer would win the opening lead on the board and immediately finesse in trump. Upon winning the trump King, West would lead a second Spade and seal Declarer's fate. As soon as Declarer tried to establish Diamonds for a discard, the defence would get their three tricks in the side suits and our hapless Declarer would bemoan his bad luck. Luck played no part in defeat of the contract. If looking for an explanation, Declarer had only to look in a mirror. All Declarer had to do to succeed was lead a Diamond at trick two.

2) EIGHT EVER, NINE NEVER

One of the many pitfalls of Bridge for newer players is their penchant for taking finesses. Once they've learned this ploy they become so enamoured with finessing that they can hardly wait to try their next one. Yet, they eventually realize that a finesse is only a 50/50 proposition and begin looking at other roads to success. While frequently needing to finesse against Kings, you have only one option for doing so – towards the A/Q if these two cards are in the same hand. However, when the Queen is the missing honour, Declarer has a more difficult decision to make since it can be picked up when in the hand of either defender. Here are some examples to illustrate this dilemma.

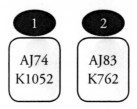

In #1, you can finesse in either direction. Unless you have gleaned something from the bidding or play to the point where the decision has to be made, it becomes a guess. In #2, you have no choice. The proper technique in this case is to cash the King and lead towards A/J. When you have only eight cards, there is a way to increase your chances of success.

> AJ74
> K1092

By exchanging the 5 for the 9 so that (1) looks like this, you can employ a technique called *'Tempt-A-Cover'*. Lead the 10 or Jack.

If the one you lead isn't covered go up with the high card on the opposite side and then finesse through the other defender. This tactic often succeeds because many players cannot resist covering an honour and getting two of Declarer's honours for one of theirs. Now back to our rhyming couplet or whatever it is. When your combined holding is nine cards, finessing for the Queen may not be necessary. When there are five cards missing, as is the case when you have eight, they normally split 3/2 making a finesse for the missing Queen is a better proposition than playing for the drop. However, when only four are missing, because your total is nine, dropping the Queen by playing your Ace and King is a slightly better percentage play. A nine card holding, without the Queen, might look like this:

AJ963
K752

Of course, if you replaced the seven with the ten, you might like to play 'Tempt-A-Cover'. The opportunity to present a simplified explanation of likely card divisions has surfaced by this point. And far be it from me, a retired teacher, to not 'strike while the iron is hot!' For too many Bridge players, remembering the percentages for these likely divisions of missing cards is difficult. It's simpler, although not as precise but close enough, to turn the number of missing cards into a common fraction. Thus, five missing cards will divide 3 – 2, two thirds of the time and 4 – 1 one quarter of the time.

Another simplified approach is that an even number of cards (6 or 4) will divide unevenly (4 – 2 or 3 – 1) more often, while an odd number of missing cards (7, 5 or 3) will divide as evenly as possible (4 – 3, 3 – 2 or 2 – 1) more frequently.

As you examine the following hands, be aware that whether or not to take a finesse is seldom your only decision. You must also consider what might happen if you lost the finesse. For example, you don't want a losing finesse to put the dangerous opponent on lead. That's the one who can then cash some tricks or lead through your unprotected honour. Therefore, while finessing with eight cards or playing for the drop when holding nine is the percentage play, there are often other factors to consider. Following are a couple of hands to illustrate the need to expand your thinking as Declarer.

*When In Doubt,
Take The Time To
Figure It Out.*

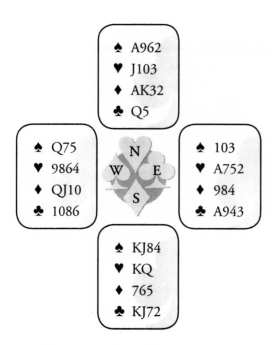

Contract: 4♠
Opening Lead: ♦Q

Declarer has natural losers in each of the side suits. So if the Spade finesse loses, the contract will be defeated. Since there is a second stopper in Diamonds, the suit which has been attacked on the opening lead, Declarer should utilize the extra Heart winner rather than bank everything on a trump finesse. After winning the opening lead, Declarer should attack Hearts immediately. By establishing the extra Heart winner in dummy, there will be a parking place for the Diamond loser. Then even if the trump finesse loses, the contract is secure.

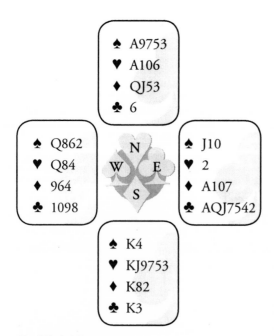

Contract: 5♥
Opening Lead: ♣10

A good 'Rule of Thumb' when missing a key honour in any suit is to arbitrarily place it in the hand of a defender whose partner has shown a long suit. It would be quite logical to assume that, after East opens a Club and bids all the way to the five level with no encouragement from West that East has a long suit. Placing that missing trump Queen with West is based on the logic that, since East has many Clubs, his hand has less room for Hearts than does his partner. That being the case, rather than playing for the drop, Declarer finesses West for the Queen.

3) PARTNER'S SUIT

Quite often, when dealing with the play in partner's suit, I am asked if my advice deals with a suit partner has bid or led. So, let's deal with both. First a suit partner has bid. One of those moth-eaten myths of yesteryear suggests that, on the opening lead you should be laying down your highest card in partner's suit. And yet, nothing could be farther from the truth. On a recent foray within my Bridge library, I happened to be thumbing through one of the master's books. In it Goren himself, 60 years ago, condemns such foolishness. It is much more important for partner to know how many cards you hold in his suit rather than which is the highest. Following are some examples of how following such archaic advice can cost your side in the currency of Bridge – tricks.

1.

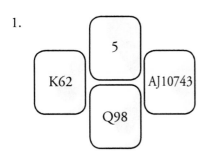

Following that downright fool-hardy advice, partner leads the King in your suit. Congratulations, you just developed a trick for Declarer – a trick which was totally undeserved. Had you treated this suit (partner's) like any other, you would have led third highest and Declarer would never have made the Queen. Except for a couple of exceptions which will be illustrated shortly, leads in partner's suit should not be any different than those in other suits.

2.

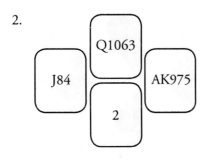

This example really drives home this advice. If a follower of the 'Highest' school, partner will lead the Jack. It will be covered by the Queen and won by your King. If you then tried to cash the Ace (not the mark of a good defender)

it would be trumped and dummy's 10 would become a trick. Once again, congratulations! You've taken exactly one trick in a suit where your side held the Ace, King and Jack with the two top honours poised over dummy's Queen. You've just graduated from the 'Bridge Magician School'. You can make tricks disappear.

1.

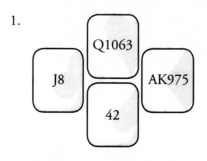

Here is the first of those exceptions mentioned earlier. In the example which was just examined, let's take the 4 from West and give it to South. This time, partner leads the Jack which is in keeping with the standard practice of leading the highest in partner's suit only if it is a Doubleton. Normally, leading a Doubleton honour in a side suit is a losing strategy but is the accepted wisdom in partner's suit. In this scenario, East knows that partner has a Doubleton at most and can cash both top honours before giving partner a ruff.

2. And here is the other exception. With a holding such as this – J1052 – more experienced defenders will lead fourth highest. However, in partner's suit, it is better to lead the top of touching honours.

Now to the returning of a suit which partner has led. One of the difficulties in which the newer players seem to find themselves far too often is blocking a suit. By this is meant that one of the defenders has a good card(s) to cash but can't because partner won the last trick in that suit. And this is why, when returning partner's suit there are guidelines which must be followed. Here's said guideline. If you originally held four cards in the suit which partner led, return the lowest one remaining. If you originally held three, return the highest one remaining. Of course, if you only had one or two originally, you'd have no choice. Following this particular advice not only prevents a blockage, it also helps partner in counting Declarer's hand. Similar advice to Declarer has been to play the high card from the short side first when planning to run an established suit. Now let's look at a complete hand to illustrate how following such dubious advice as always returning partner's suit is a losing strategy. And although breaking a new suit is normally unwise, there are exceptions to this guideline just as there are with all of those Bridge rules. However, when breaking this one, defender is actually abiding by another – leading up to weakness.

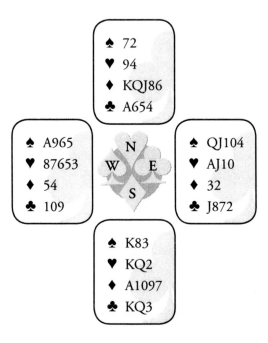

Contract: 3N.T.
Opening Lead: ♥8

With some help, Declarer has nine easy tricks – five ♦, three ♣ and given the opening lead, one ♥. The help would come in the form of a return of partner's suit, by R.H.O., after winning trick one with the Ace. Without that helpful return but a switch to the ♠Queen, the defence takes the first five tricks. So much for the myth of returning partner's suit. By doing so, in this case, it would have handed Declarer the contract.

However, don't always be guided by the myth or be loathe to do it based on any one hand. Each hand should be defended based on its own merits. Perhaps a little levity would be in order at this point. The following was on a T-shirt at a tournament:

Two reasons why I don't return partner's suit:
1. I don't have any
2. I don't like this partner

4 & 5) SECOND HAND LOW & THIRD HAND HIGH

I like to call these twin myths. These two probably have the most exceptions. *'Second Hand Low'* simply means that you should play a low card in second seat when the dummy or Declarer is on your right and leads. The logic behind this guideline is that third hand will likely play a high card in an effort to win the trick, so you shouldn't waste a high card in second seat. This advice is considered a myth because to live and die by it when it has so many exceptions is a losing strategy. And its twin *'Third Hand High'*, which simply means playing a high card in third seat when partner has led to the trick, is also a myth with many exceptions. In the following card combinations we'll examine how each of these statements has merit, but also why they shouldn't replace thinking. And although consideration of the complete hand will often govern how an individual suit should be handled, complete hands are not needed to illustrate these two myths.

First to the advice of *'Second Hand Low'*. As stated, playing a high card in second seat is usually a losing strategy since third hand will likely play a high card. In these isolated suits, you are in second seat when Declarer leads toward dummy.

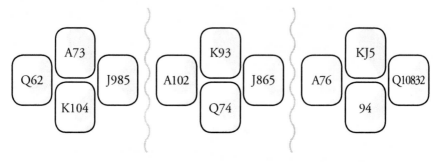

In each of the above examples, Declarer leads the four, and in each case playing *'Second Hand Low'* wins the day.

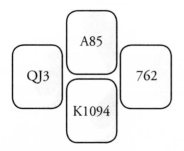

However, as can be seen in these examples when Declarer leads small, *'Second Hand Low'* would be unwise. You might be giving Declarer an extra trick or allowing an end play. In the first of these two, Declarer gets an extra trick if you play low. In the second, you could be end played if you wait for the second round to take your Ace. To prevent a possible end play, take your Ace on the first round and return the suit.

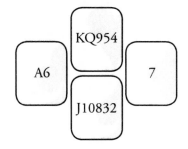

And now *'Third Hand High'*. It is very often the case when Declarer or dummy leads and you are second to play that you have very little information about partner's hand. You are therefore in a much more difficult position and more inclined to obey the myths. However, when you are playing to a trick in third seat, partner has led and if the two of you are disciplined – and that is an absolute – your play in that third seat becomes more purposeful. For whatever reason partner has led a suit, be that on the opening lead or a subsequent trick, the specific card has to by convention. For example, if partner leads a small card, it is likely from one or two non-touching honours. Applying the *'Rule of 11'* will enlighten you. If that low card could be top of a Doubleton, not only will the *'Rule of 11'* reveal some incongruity but the number of cards held by you and dummy will make recognizing it as a worthless Doubleton very possible. Of course, that low card could be from three cards with something valuable at the top. Remember *'BOSTON'*. And once you have interpreted that lead, your play in third seat becomes simpler so that not living by that *'Third Hand High'* myth is no longer so unthinking.

Learn The Rules And When To Break Them.

Here are some examples of this particular command of yesteryear being advisable and not so requiring of compliance.

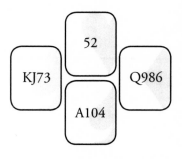

Partner leads the 3. Applying the *Rule of 11* reveals that Declarer has three cards in the suit that are higher than the three. Because you can see the 2 in dummy means partner can only have four cards in the suit because fourth highest leads are quite common. So, knowing that partner has one or two non-touching honours, what could it or they be? Partner doesn't have the Ace unless this is a N.T. contract. Let's assume it is a suit contract. Therefore, partner can't have the Ace. Nor does he have the A/K or he would have led one of them depending on your agreement. Partner can't have the K/Q because you have the Queen and he would have led the King from those two touching honours. And partner couldn't have the J/10 because he might have led the Jack although this not a universally accepted lead. From K/J/10, partner very likely would lead the Jack. Having taken all this into consideration will lead you to the conclusion that partner has led fourth highest from one of these three holdings, Kxxx, KJxx, Jxxx, K10xx. Whichever the case may be, you must play third hand high and contribute the Queen to the trick.

And this is why leads must be disciplined. Although it takes a minute or so to read all that you've just read, these thoughts will flash through your brain in a matter of seconds when at the table.

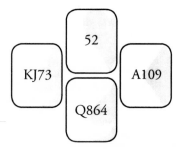

Here's another example of why *Third Hand High* is often the correct play. In this case all we've done is exchange Declarer's hand with his R.H.O. and change one card. If the player on the right doesn't play the Ace when partner leads the 3, Declarer wins an undeserved trick with the Queen.

However, one must not become dogmatic and routinely play high in third seat without having first analysed partner's lead. Here are some examples of why following such advice without putting some thought into it is a losing strategy.

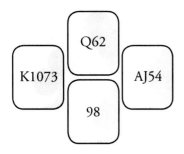

Putting on your thinking cap once again, will lead you to the conclusion that partner, having led the 3, has either the King or 10 or both. That being the case, you must play your Jack, shunning the dogmatic play of the Ace. This play is the winning strategy if partner has any of the three possible holdings. If Declarer has the King, he'll be held to one trick while playing the Ace will establish both the King and Queen as tricks. And if Declarer has the 10, your Jack will win.

Being Satisfied Prevents Learning.

Here's another.

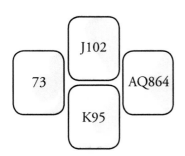

If you suspect partner is leading a worthless Doubleton don't take the first trick. If you or partner can win a trick before Declarer clears the trump suit, a ruff can be arranged in the suit.

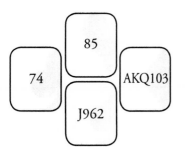

Look at this example. It is a rather specialized case of not playing high in third seat so as to maintain communication with partner. It is much the same ploy as Declarer ducking a trick to preserve entries. Partner leads the 7 in your suit. Suspecting a Doubleton, you cover dummy's 8 with the 10. Declarer wins this trick but you eventually score four tricks in the suit. Yes Gertrude, this is a 3N.T. contract. What you've done is left partner with a card in your suit so that partner will then be able to lead your suit again when he gains the lead. Of course, so much the better if you eventually gain the lead in another suit. So, don't let these two relics replace thinking.

6) COVER AN HONOUR

This is one of those myths that has survived from yesteryear. Many aspiring Bridge players think it to be one of those absolutes which might lead to banishment from the game if not followed religiously. After all, who would be foolish enough not to jump at a two-for-one sale. And that is precisely what you are accomplishing when you follow this advice – two of Declarer's honours for one of yours. However, the real purpose of such a ploy is to promote a trick for either defender. Unfortunately, doing so makes life easier for Declarer much more often than it develops tricks for the defenders. Let's first look at why such advice has survived since the days of whist. Players tend to remember how covering has occasionally been successful but tend to forget the many times it was not. Here are some of those happier times.

1.

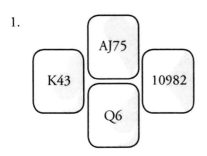

If Declarer leads the Queen and you don't cover (play your King), the Queen will win and a subsequent finesse of the Jack will produce three tricks for Declarer. Had you covered (played your King), Declarer would have been held to two tricks because partner's 10 and 9 would become master cards.

2.

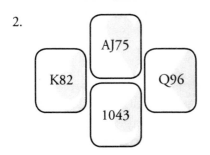

Suppose Declarer leads the 10 – not a good play without the 9 – and you don't cover. The Queen will win but a subsequent finesse of the Jack, with the suit splitting favourably for Declarer, will get Declarer three tricks. Yet, if you had covered with your King on that first trick, Declarer would have realized only two and then only if there was a side entry to dummy.

3. If you cover the 9 with the 10, Declarer can be held to one trick. If you don't cover it, the 9 will run to partner's Queen and when Declarer then finesses the Jack, he has a second trick. And if the card combinations looked like the second example, Declarer

would have three tricks by your not covering the 9.

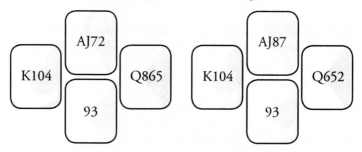

It's examples like the three above that have convinced defenders that covering an honour with an honour is the only thing good players can do. And that not covering is the mark of a very poor player.

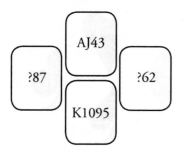

Yet there are far more times when not covering is really the mark of a very good player. One of the favourite ploys of a Declarer who has a two-way finesse for a Queen is to Tempt-A-Cover. Declarer will lead the Jack from dummy or the 10 from his hand. If second hand covers, which is what too many would do, Declarer's problem is solved. And if the card led isn't covered Declarer will go up and finesse through the other hand. Since you are a member of the 'cover' school and didn't, it's because you don't have the damsel.

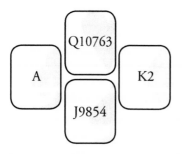

Another poor result occurs when an honour is covered if it catches a Singleton honour in partner's hand. The classic example of this blunder is the old story of Declarer making a small slam missing the Ace and King of trump. Here's the trump holding. Declarer leads the Queen from dummy and second hand covers. End of story.

Another example of how covering helps Declarer is the lead from a Doubleton honour in dummy, although it could also be from Declarer's hand. A good Declarer will not lead a Queen unless he also has the Jack – there might be

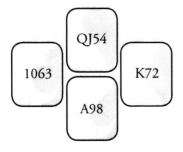

isolated cases where he might lead the Queen and not be in possession of the Jack. Dummy leads the Queen. If you cover, Declarer can now pick up partner's 10. The rule is to wait for the Jack to be led before covering, thus protecting partner's 10. And if partner doesn't have the 10, your cause is hopeless regardless of what you do.

One last example of the foolishness of covering is best seen in a complete hand.

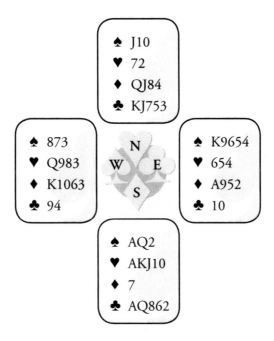

Contract: 6♣   Opening Lead: ♦3

This hand illustrates one of the similar Declarer techniques which allow Declarer to test one line of play and still be able to fall back on the second if the first is unsuccessful. And that's the option of trying to drop a Queen when Declarer and dummy have nine cards in a suit before finessing for a missing damsel in another suit where the two hands have only eight cards.

In the hand pictured above, Declarer can tempt a defender to cover an honour in one suit and if said offender resists the temptation or can't cover, Declarer can win and then try the finesse in a second suit. Here, Declarer can lead the Spade Jack from dummy. If it is covered, the Spade loser has been eliminated and Declarer can try the Heart finesse for an overtrick. If the Spade play doesn't succeed, a successful Heart finesse becomes a necessity.

Mae West Was Supposed To Have Said, "Avoid Temptation Unless It is Irresistible."

7) SPLIT YOUR HONOURS

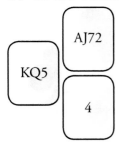

Splitting your honours simply means that if you have touching honours and R.H.O. leads towards a higher one, you should play one of yours to prevent said opponent from winning a cheap trick. When the 4 is led, play the Queen – you are said to be splitting your honours – so that Declarer doesn't win a cheap trick with the Jack. Notice the mention of specifically the Queen. When splitting your honours, play the lower. Partner will then be reasonably certain that you have the King. If you split them by playing the King first, partner wouldn't realize that you have the Queen. Splitting honours is not a guaranteed road to success but on average is the best you can do. This is basically the same principle as playing the lower of touching honours, in third seat, when partner leads small and second hand plays small. Here are some other examples of how to handle your touching honours.

1.

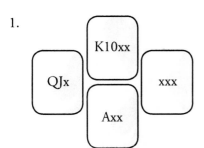

Declarer leads a spot toward the K/10. Play your Jack and be assured of a trick. Duck and you'll get none.

2.

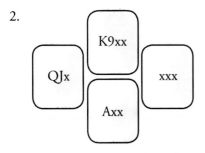

Here's a little deception which might steer Declarer in the wrong direction. This is trump and you are making the opening lead. Lead the Jack. Declarer might think that you are one of those players who likes to lead Singleton trump and finesse partner for the Queen. You're still splitting your honours. Although splitting your honours, as mentioned, is normally your best move be aware that there are pitfalls.

3.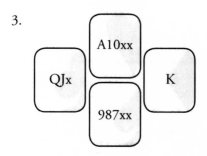

When Declarer leads a small card toward the A/10, splitting the Q/J might bring down your partner's Singleton honour. That's two of yours for one of theirs – not a good trade. Of course, if partner doesn't have the King and you don't split, guess who'll win the post mortem?

4. By splitting you might simplify play for Declarer. The normal play for Declarer holding A – J – 9 opposite three spots is to finesse the 9, playing the defender who plays before the hand with these cards to hold K/10 or Q/10. If you were that defender and split your honours, Declarer would be able to lead toward the Jack, once the Queen and Ace had been played and get a second trick. Yet if you didn't split them and Declarer did finesse, losing to the 10, he would be held to one trick.

Advice From Yesteryear Doesn't Replace Thinking

8) RUFF AND SLUFF

As a defender, giving a *'Ruff and Scuff'* is considered such a heinous crime that it is second only to trumping a partner's Ace or failing to lead partner's suit. And, although such a poor defensive mistake has, as does everything else in this humbling game, dire consequences, it occasionally is a winning strategy. First, let's understand what this defensive blunder is actually costing the defence. Quite often, when Declarer has a loser in the dummy as well as his own hand, the lead of a suit, by a defender, in which both Declarer and dummy are void allows Declarer to trump on one side while discarding a loser from the opposite hand. But, as mentioned above, there are times when it is the only positive approach that a defender can take. Allowing a Declarer such an opportunity is really not a blunder in the following cases:

- Aiding in the set up of a suit

- Declarer hasn't a loser to discard

- Avoid breaking a new suit

- Promotes a trump trick for the defence

However, what would a list of rules in this game be without those ubiquitous caveats. And here's the one which pertains here. Before allowing a *'Ruff and Sluff'*, no harm will befall the defence, if all the tricks to which defenders are entitled have been taken. This is much the same as the prerequisite required of Declarer when planning to cross-ruff a hand. Declarer must first cash all side suit winners before embarking on a cross-ruff. If Declarer has not taken those side suit winners first, a defender, when unable to over ruff or follow suit, will be discarding from another suit. When Declarer tries to then cash those side suit winners, guess what that dastardly defender will do? In the two hands which follow, we'll examine how devastating a *'Ruff and Sluff'* can be to the defence, as well as how it can sometimes be helpful.

Acceptable If Declarer Has Only Winners

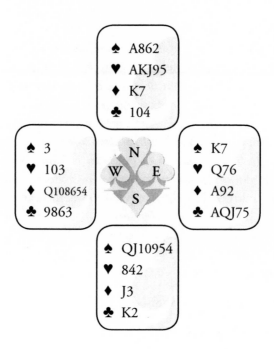

Contract: 4♠   Opening Lead: ♣9

From Declarers standpoint, there are five losers given the opening lead. However, East does not know that he will soon be aiding and abetting the enemy. After winning the opening lead, East led a Club which was won by Declarer's King. At this point, Declarer led the Ace and a second trump, losing to the King. And now, not wanting to lead a Heart or a Diamond which would hand Declarer a free finesse, East led a Club. This allowed Declarer to discard a Heart while trumping in dummy. Now two rounds of Hearts and a third round ruff allowed Declarer to pitch his Diamond losers on the fourth and fifth Hearts. The entry to dummy was a trump to the 8.

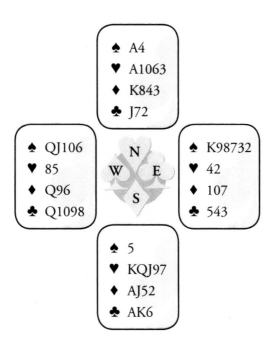

Contract: 6♥   Opening Lead: ♠Q

It would appear that Declarer has a Club and Diamond loser. However as good Declarers are wont to do, our hero sets upon a course to enlist the aid of a hapless defender. Declarer wins the opening lead and ruffs a Spade, eliminating that suit. He then draws trump, eliminating a second suit. By cashing A/K of Clubs and leading a third round, Declarer simultaneously eliminates a third suit and throws the lead to a defender. Said defender is now at the crossroads of the hand. If he leads a Diamond, breaking a new suit which most defenders are loathe to do, Declarer is handed the slam. So, West must take a chance by giving Declarer a *'Ruff and Sluff'*. A slim chance is better than none. In this instance, giving a *'Ruff and Sluff'* is not a losing play because it does Declarer no good.

GUIDELINES

A Lightly Drawn Line Used as a Guide

*"The more things change,
the more they stay the same."*

This is a statement we've all heard before. As it applies to Bridge, even though the game has changed greatly over the years, it simply means that advice of yesteryear in many cases still holds true today. The following is an example, from a book published in 1904, which gives Bridge tips that haven't changed over the years.

THE
LAWS AND PRINCIPLES
of
BRIDGE
STATED AND EXPLAINED
and the
PRACTICE ILLUSTRATED
HANDS PLAYED COMPLETELY THROUGH.
BY
"HELLESPONT"

FOURTH EDITION.

LONDON
THOS. DE LA RUE & CO. Ltd
1904

HINTS ON THE GENERAL PLAY OF THE GAME.

It sometimes becomes apparent, after a few tricks have been played at "no trumps," that unless your partner holds some particular card or cards, you cannot save the game. In such positions you must assume him to hold that card or cards and play accordingly, even though this necessitates your sacrificing a winning card in your hand. For instance, you get the lead pretty late in the hand, and hold the king and a small club. The queen and two others are in the exposed hand. You require three tricks to save the game, and, unless your partner holds the ace, knave, and one or more clubs, you cannot get them. You must lead the king, on the assumption that he has these cards.

You should always closely observe the tactics adopted by the dealer. If he avoids opening any particular suit, of which the Dummy holds some good cards, you may assume that he is weak in it, and that your partner holds some of the missing cards. Likewise, if he plays a cautious game, by avoiding finesses and securing tricks at once, you may take it that he is not very strong, or that your partner has some powerful suit against him. When the declaration is left, and an offensive trump is declared, if the dealer leaves trumps alone, he is either very weak, or he wants to ruff from his own hand.

Remember that the dealer will always play his cards with intent to deceive his adversaries, and you must not be deterred from continuing, with a winning card in a suit, merely because he has dropped a high card on the previous trick.

When your partner deals, lay down your hand at once, and without any remark, as soon as a card is led. Spread the cards out, so that they are most conveniently visible, and then lapse into your position as Dummy.

Always play as quickly as you can, and avoid talking. It is difficult to say which is the most exasperating—an undecided, hesitating, and deliberative player, or a garrulous and babbling one. A combination of the two is too insufferable for words.

Avoid continually asking to look at the last trick. It should seldom be necessary if you are attending to the game.

Always give your partner a ruff whenever you get the chance; you cannot force him too often at Bridge. At the same time, always force the strong adverse trump hand, unless by doing so you play the dealer's game, or unless it is so strong that the force is welcome.

Always make the trick that saves the game when you have the chance, or you may never make it.

If you throw away all the cards of your partner's suit when there are no trumps, you indicate to him that you have no card of entry.

Never, unless it cannot deceive your partner, play a false card, except as dealer. This prohibition is even more imperative without trumps than when there are trumps.

As dealer, play false cards whenever you can.

Never, in discarding, when there are no trumps, denude yourself entirely of a suit unless you can never get the lead. If you do, you not only are unable to lead it to your partner, should it in turn out to be his strong suit, but you also enable the dealer, as soon as it is led, to locate the whole of it, and to finesse accordingly.

Never risk the game in the hope of making extra points; and always play in such a way as to make it easy for your partner.

Always note carefully the fall of every card. It often happens that an inattentive player will fail to recollect that his eight or nine is the best of the suit remaining, because he has omitted to observe the fall of the nine or ten.

1) HOLD-UP OR DUCK

Although to *'Duck'* or *'Hold-Up'* would seem synonymous, they are so only in the technique itself but differ in their application. Ducking is done in your own suit either to conserve or establish entries or to help set-up a suit. You *'Hold-Up'* in their suit, most likely to sever communications between defenders. A *'Hold-Up'* might be considered a defensive maneuver while ducking would be offensive in nature. The following two hands will show Declarer holding-up as a defensive technique and ducking as an offensive ploy. Also, since establishing a suit for discards is a very valuable Declarer technique that isn't utilized by enough Declarers, let's examine how a *'Hold-Up'* can help in this particular technique. Then we'll look at how a *'Duck'* can allow you to conserve entries.

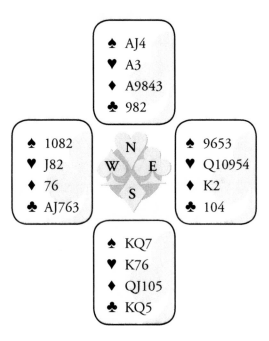

    ♠ AJ4
    ♥ A3
    ♦ A9843
    ♣ 982

♠ 1082   ♠ 9653
♥ J82   ♥ Q10954
♦ 76   ♦ K2
♣ AJ763   ♣ 104

    ♠ KQ7
    ♥ K76
    ♦ QJ105
    ♣ KQ5

Contract: 3N.T.   Opening Lead: ♣6

It should be obvious to even newer players that Declarer needs to bring in some Diamond tricks to reach the goal of 3N.T. Yet, that involves the need for a successful finesse of the King or failing that to exhaust R.H.O. of Clubs so that a Club return by said opponent does not spell disaster. Since Declarer only needs one Club trick, all Declarer has to do is duck the first Club. When the Diamond finesse loses, R.H.O. will have no Club to return.

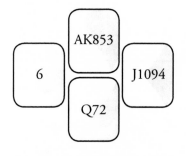

To illustrate a *'duck'* we need only an isolated suit and not a complete hand. If all five tricks are needed from this suit, Declarer must cash the Queen and lead to the Ace or King. That's in keeping with the principles of high card from the short side first. However, if only four tricks are required and there are no other entries to the long hand, a safety play is in order. Lead the Queen and then duck a round of the suit. Even if the suit breaks 4 – 1 as in this case, four tricks are assured. Admittedly, playing this way costs a trick if the suit breaks 3 – 2 which is normal. It's the situation which makes safety plays much more suited to rubber Bridge than duplicate. In duplicate, that fifth trick is worth its weight in gold – duplicate players would prefer to receive their reward in master points.

2) EXTRA WINNERS

1.

♠ K83
♥ Q765
♦ K10
♣ J1075

♠ A54
♥ AJ109
♦ Q6
♣ Q862

One of the many frustrating things about Bridge is discovering that you have nothing but mirrored suits. Mirrored suits are suits which have the same number of cards on each side of the table. For example, this hand is all mirrored suits – three ♠, four ♥, two ♦ and four ♣ in each. This state of affairs can be detrimental to Declarer's cause. Since Declarer's basic ways of eliminating losers is to trump them in dummy or to discard them on an established suit or extra winners, mirrored suits effectively eliminate two of those three. This hand has 24 H.C.P. The two following hands also have 24 H.C.P. yet the comparative trick taking power of the three hands is vastly different.

2.

♠ KQ2
♥ J107654
♦ 3
♣ A76

♠ A5
♥ K
♦ KQJ108752
♣ J4

Hand #1, regardless of the contract, will likely take six or seven tricks. Hand #2, playing Diamonds, can take 11 tricks as long as Declarer uses the extra Spade winner to dispose of one of the losers in his hand – either a Heart or a Club. And this is the advantage of having an un-mirrored suit with those high cards. Hand #3, playing in Hearts can take ten tricks after Declarer disposes of a Diamond or Spade loser on the extra Club winner. This is the value of extra winners in a suit. And there can only be extra winners in a suit which is not mirrored. However, watch the timing. In hand #2, trying to pull trump immediately could be suicidal. If the opening lead had been a Club, dislodging your only stopper in that suit, losing a trump lead to the Ace would see defenders quickly cashing a Heart and a Club to hold Declarer to ten tricks. Don't be too quick to lead trump if you can't afford to lose the lead. In hand #3, leading trump would not cause Declarer to lose the lead so drawing trump first would be prudent.

3.

♠ A65
♥ Q1083
♦ J109
♣ AQ4

♠ 753
♥ AKJ652
♦ 63
♣ K5

It's results like these that confirm how fits and not H.C.P. are responsible for the success of most contracts. In these preceding examples, Declarer was discarding losers on winners in the dummy. Doing so is a step in the right direction. However, discarding losers from the dummy is also a step in the right direction but with a slight detour. The following hand illustrates just such a detour.

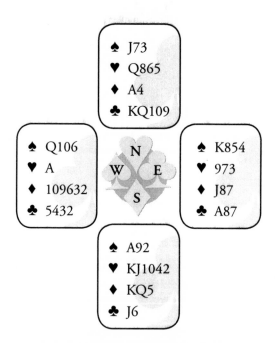

♠ J73
♥ Q865
♦ A4
♣ KQ109

♠ Q106
♥ A
♦ 109632
♣ 5432

N
W E
S

♠ K854
♥ 973
♦ J87
♣ A87

♠ A92
♥ KJ1042
♦ KQ5
♣ J6

Contract: 4♥   Opening Lead: ♦10

The losers in this hand would appear to be 2 ♠, a trump and a Club. However, there is an extra winner in Diamonds. Unfortunately, it is in the long hand (Declarer's). As a result, this necessitates a two stage process. The first trick should be won in dummy and a second Diamond led to the King. On the third Diamond trick a Spade can be discarded from dummy. This enables

Declarer to trump a Spade loser in dummy and condense four losers into three. Although it is unlikely that the third Diamond would be trumped, Declarer would be wise to first draw trump. There would still be a trump in dummy to ruff the third round of Spades.

If the trump happened to be split 4 – 0, Declarer, upon regaining the lead could go about playing the Diamonds and ruffing a Spade before completing the task of drawing trump. Reference has been made about not drawing trump if Declarer cannot afford to lose the lead. However, in this case, losing the lead to the trump Ace is not a problem since there is no return which the defender can make to sink the contract.

3) Ruff In Dummy

As can be readily seen from the following trump holding, Declarer would be entitled to five trump tricks. However, if Declarer were to trump a loser in dummy before drawing trump, he would make six trump tricks and by trumping a second loser in dummy that total would increase to seven. Trumping a third loser in dummy would make eight trump tricks. As can also be seen, trumping in the long hand (that's the one with the greater number of trump), although it might be necessary, doesn't increase your total trump tricks. Although this technique is basic to good Declarer play there are times when it is a losing strategy, just like the exceptions to any guideline in this game. By adhering to this philosophy at all costs, you might block yourself in dummy and not be able to draw trump. You might need them as entries when establishing a suit for discards. And a *'Dummy Reversal'* might be your only salvation. For those unfamiliar with this term it simply means trumping in the long hand and using dummy's trump to draw those held by defenders. As will immediately be realized this reverses the normal procedure of trumping in dummy and drawing the enemy's trump with Declarer's long hand. Hence the name *'Dummy Reversal'.* However, this can only be achieved if dummy's trump are strong enough to get the job done. It might even be necessary to utilize a finesse to accomplish this goal. Following is a hand which illustrates this seemingly mind-boggling technique.

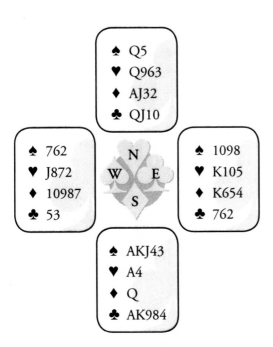

Contract: 7♣
Opening Lead: ♦10

Seeing a potential Heart loser, the unthinking Declarer will duck the opening lead, thinking that by winning with the ♦Queen, he will then be able to discard the Heart loser on dummy's ♦Ace – curtains. "Holy high cards Batman," Robin might be heard to utter. Most Declarers would chalk this up to bad luck and move on to the next deal, without realizing that the hand cannot be defeated if Declarer handles his assets properly.

Although plays such as coups, squeezes, etcetera, are thought to be the domain of experts, they really aren't. And as mentioned, one such technique, namely a dummy reversal, is Declarer's salvation on this hand. The problem with utilizing this technique is not in the execution but in recognizing the need to employ it and then having the necessary resources. So, after examining and then rejecting other options as losing strategies, Declarer has to look elsewhere. And that elsewhere is a dummy reversal. An absolute requirement is that dummy has to be the hand which draws defender's trump. Therefore, if dummy is unable to do this, forget the dummy reversal. In this hand, Declarer wins trick one in dummy and ruffs a Diamond with a high trump. A trump is led to dummy and a second Diamond is trumped high. Another trump is led to dummy and the last Diamond is trumped with Declarer's last trump. Declarer then leads a Spade to dummy and on dummy's last trump discards the losing Heart. The remaining tricks go to Declarer's Heart and Spades.

4) SAFETY PLAY

Before delving into specifics of this topic, let's examine the meaning as well as the potential use of this play. For example, bad suit breaks can sink a contract as can a dangerous opponent gaining the lead. These are but two of the circumstances of which a competent Declarer will be aware. As will be seen in the following hand a Declarer executing a safety play is simply taking out insurance against one of these unpleasant occurrences. When to use a safety play is really in the form of a caveat. A safety play has much to recommend it if playing rubber Bridge or IMP scoring. In both of these forms of Bridge making the contract is the prime consideration. However, if playing pairs in a duplicate game where beating the other pairs is uppermost in the minds of Declarers, using a safety play might result in a bad result. After all, a safety play often results in the loss of a trick. This is a trick which a less diligent Declarer might not lose, resulting in a somewhat undeserved good result.

Good Players Don't Always Make The Tough Hands, They Simply Don't Mess Up The Easy Ones.

And now the hand.

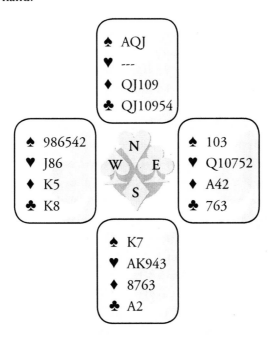

Contract: 3N.T.   Opening Lead: ♠5

With only six top tricks Declarer had to find three more. Although the Club suit could provide more than enough tricks to bring in 3N.T., Declarer had to be careful. He couldn't waste a Spade entry to dummy in order to try a Club finesse. Therefore, leading Ace and another Club was the winning strategy. However, if Declarer won the opening lead in his hand and proceeded to play the Clubs in this manner, he would be locked on the board with only eight tricks. His A/K of Hearts would be an unreachable 9th and 10th tricks. Yet if Declarer cashed the top Hearts before attacking Clubs, good defenders would end up with three ♥, a ♣ and two ♦. But a good Declarer asks the question, "What can go wrong?" and proceeds to take countermeasures. Instead of cashing both Hearts, Declarer cashed only one, thereby sacrificing the overtrick (a safety play) and proceeded to gather nine tricks. However, to ensure that the safety play didn't actually work to Declarer's advantage, the defenders had to play cautiously and not break a new suit after winning the Club. If the defence led a Heart, that would be Declarer's 10th trick and a Diamond followed by a second would also give Declarer an overtrick. Upon winning the ♣King, that defender must lead a Spade.

5) TOWARDS HIGH CARDS

There are a multitude of guidelines in the game and there are a multitude of exceptions. However, this guideline would seem to have fewer of those expletive exceptions. And although seeing complete hands is the best way to view most techniques, this guideline is just as easily explained by viewing isolated suits. Here are some basic situations which arise quite frequently.

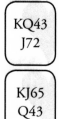

These holdings are identical for our purposes. Lead small towards the side with two honours. If second hand has the Ace and is forced to play it without capturing an honour, you'll have three tricks. This is the best way to make more than two. And if the Ace was in the other defender's hand so that the distribution of cards looked like this, the only way to bring in three tricks is to lead through the hand which you suspected had the Ace. If the Jack in the first example or the Queen in the second were to win that first trick, you could then play small from both hands and hope the Ace had been part of a Doubleton. In the preceding examples, Declarer has the K/Q/J in his possession.

In this example, Declarer only has the King and Queen but both on the same side. Once again, lead towards the double honour. If the Ace is Doubleton on the left, leading twice from the bottom hand will result in three tricks.

The following are more basic examples and are more easily recognized by beginning players. In these leading away from the high cards is a losing proposition, while leading towards them is the winning strategy.

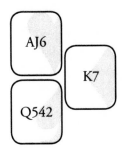

Here is an exception to the guidelines of leading towards high cards. If you have reason to believe that the King is to the right, the only hope for three tricks from this suit is to hope it is Doubleton. Lead the 6. Finessing by leading towards the A/J will produce only two.

6) TOUCHING HONOURS

This is another of those areas where newer players really get confused. The handling of touching honours can vary depending, not only when declaring or defending, but also by your location at the table. Here are some examples of this touchy problem.

1. **K/Qx (x)** If defending when holding this combination, you would lead the top of touching honours but if following, in third seat, to partner's lead of a small card you would play the Queen, if dummy played low. It's no wonder that the play of this combination is confusing to many. Even the explanation is.

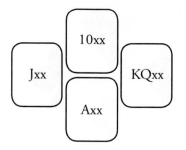

A visual explanation should help. When partner leads a small card and dummy contributes a little card, play your Queen. When it forces Declarer to play the Ace, partner will know that you hold the King. If you play the King, forcing Declarer to play the Ace, partner wouldn't know that you held the Queen.

2. **QJx (x)** With this combination, nothing would change if partner led small and dummy played a low card. You would still contribute the lower of touching honours in third seat. However, when leading this suit, there are many experienced players who would want to have the ten as well before leading the Queen.

3. **J10x (x)** Same explanation as #2.

4. **AKx (x)** Same explanation as #1. This example has been shown so that some similar yet different scenarios can be discussed.

Many players lead the King from A/K as well as from the K/Q. If partner cannot see the touching card in the dummy or his own hand, this can be confusing. Therefore, if the lead from A/K is always the Ace, then partner will know that a King led promises the Queen and denies the Ace. Yet, there are exceptions here as well. The leading principles above refer to suits other than one bid by partner.

Although leading an honour in partner's suit could be promising the lower touching card, it could also be the top card of a Doubleton such as KX, QX, etcetera. Handling A/K and K/Q differently also allows the defender on lead to show that an A/K is Doubleton or that a K/Q is also a Doubleton. By leading the King and then the Ace confirms a Doubleton.

In another section of this book, handling the combinations of lesser stature, such as Q/J and J/10, in a deceptive manner, will be discussed. And adding to the confusion for many is the fact that, as a Declarer, leading towards touching honours is almost always a winning strategy. All of the above reminds me of another Bridge book, 'Easier Done Than Said'.

7) FINESSES

Ah, finessing. What joy. These are the thoughts of the true finessaholic. See finesse, take finesse is their mantra. It never occurs to them to try the finesse acid test. What might happen if the finesse loses? The golden rule of finessing is to take a finesse if it is necessary to the success of your contract but not to if it isn't. As well, even if a finesse appears to be necessary, a competent Declarer looks at other options first and doesn't routinely rely on a finesse. In both of the hands which follow, Declarer was guilty of not asking that question. "What can go wrong if the finesse loses?"

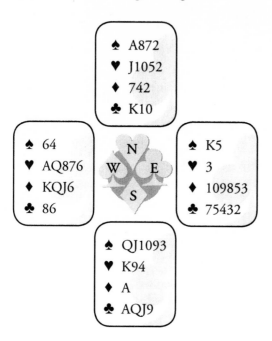

Contract: 4♠
Opening Lead: ♦K

Counting losers, Declarer can see one trump, if the King is offside and two Hearts, but only if R.H.O. is allowed on lead to send a Heart through Declarer's unprotected King. And with L.H.O. having bid Hearts during the auction, Declarer should have been sufficiently warned that trying a trump finesse would likely lead to disaster. But our Declarer was of the "See finesse, take finesse"

school and soon lost the contract and the post mortem. Admittedly L.H.O., having bid, was the odds on favourite to hold the trump King but the consequences of a losing finesse were too hard to ignore. When the smoke had cleared, Declarer had lost a Spade, two Hearts and a Heart ruff for down one. Had our hero simply led out the Ace of trump followed by a second, there would have been no Heart ruff and partner would have been cooing rather than breathing fire. Notice that, had R.H.O. been of the school which always

"If this finesse works, I promise I'll be good."

returns partner's suit (Diamonds) Declarer would have a much easier time.

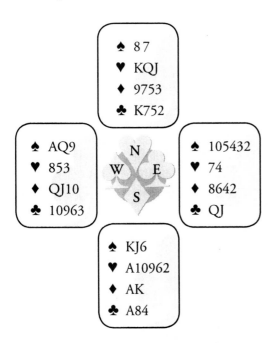

         ♠ 87
         ♥ KQJ
         ♦ 9753
         ♣ K752

♠ AQ9   ♠ 105432
♥ 853   N   ♥ 74
♦ QJ10   W   E   ♦ 8642
♣ 10963   S   ♣ QJ

         ♠ KJ6
         ♥ A10962
         ♦ AK
         ♣ A84

Contract: 4♥
Opening Lead: ♦Q

Once again, counting losers reveals one ♣ and two ♠. However, those Spade losers are only so if R.H.O. led them through the K/J. Worse still would be if Declarer perpetrated this crime on himself by leading Spades from the board. But one Declarer couldn't resist leading Spades from dummy. After all, this was a finesse and he was a card-carrying member of the F.A. (Finessaholics Anonymous).

So he led a trump to dummy and finessed a Spade. L.H.O., upon winning could see that Declarer might ruff a Spade loser or two in dummy and led a second round of trump. When the second Spade finesse lost and L.H.O. led another trump, Declarer's contract was lost. Again, guess who won the post mortem? Had Declarer simply led a Spade after winning the opening lead, the contract would have been secure. As successful Declarers know, there are four reasons for not drawing trump immediately.

1. Dummy's trump are needed for ruffing.

2. Dummy's trump are needed as entries.

3. Declarer can't afford to lose the lead.

4. Declarer needs to set up a side suit first.

In this hand, as soon as Declarer did not go after trump immediately, L.H.O. did it for him. Stop avoiding trump leads when defending. This last hand gives Declarer an alternative to a finesse. Experienced Declarers will always look for some other means of success before resorting to a finesse. They view finesses, which are only a 50/50 proposition, as a last resort.

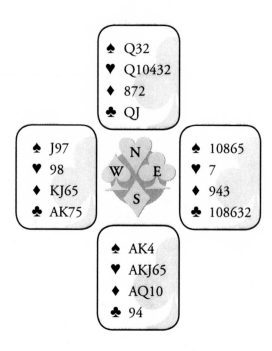

Contract: 4♥   Opening Lead: ♣A

Most Declarers, after losing the first two Club tricks and then winning the third when L.H.O. switched to a Spade, would bank everything on the Diamond finesse. They would reason that trying two finesses would be a 75% chance of success and not look further – the 100% certainty of a strip and elimination. By definition, Declarer strips the defenders of their safe exit cards and eliminates any chance of defeat. This hand is one of those dreaded collections of mirrored suits. When such a hand surfaces, Declarer should think strip and elimination. The first two Club tricks have stripped Clubs from Declarer and dummy. Although the defenders still have Clubs they can't lead them without giving Declarer a ruff and sluff. Declarer then strips the trump and Spades, ending in dummy, and leads a Diamond covering whatever R.H.O. plays. When L.H.O. wins this trick, he is West of a rock and East of a hard place. If he leads a Club, Declarer trumps in dummy and discards a Diamond from his hand. And if L.H.O. leads a Diamond Declarer gets a free finesse. In effect what Declarer has done is to force L.H.O. into a Hobson's choice.

However, be aware that there must still be trump in both hands or the ruff and sluff option is not available to Declarer.

8) THROUGH STRENGTH

Here is another situation which is greatly influenced by your location at the table. Because Declarer can see all of his assets, guidelines such as leading through strength or towards high cards are much easier to implement. Defenders, unable to see partner's hand, must rely on assumptions to utilize the same guidelines. And this is why location at the table plays such a critical role. If a defender were to see a combination such as this in dummy, leading the suit from the right (up to dummy) would be suicidal. **AQx** While leading from the left could be a winning strategy if partner had the King. But with worthless cards such **843** as these in dummy, it's leading from the left that could be suicidal, while leading from the right would now become the potentially winning strategy. In the case of the AQx, leading from the right might trap partner's King if he had it. If Declarer had it, nothing would be lost but why tempt fate. In the case of small cards in dummy, leading from the left might trap partner's good cards while leading from the right might not necessarily produce any positive results but would certainly be more palatable. Here is a complete hand to illustrate not only the advisability of leading up to weakness but also the folly of always returning partner's suit.

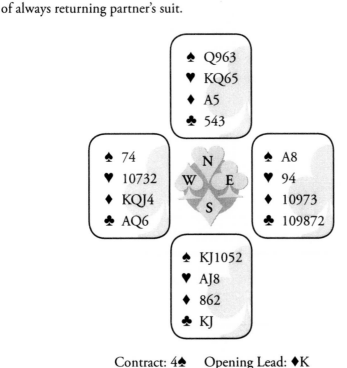

Contract: 4♠   Opening Lead: ♦K

East should see the necessary defence immediately upon taking the opening lead, Declarer will likely begin drawing trump. East should realize the futility of returning partner's suit when winning the trump Ace. There is no guarantee that a Club switch at trick three will produce enough tricks to defeat four ♠ but there is always a possibility that the switch will be successful while returning a trump would be passive and a Heart would be leading up to strength. Partner's Diamond trick will likely never go away. If leading through strength and up to weakness is difficult to remember, try this poem:

When dummy's on your right,
Lead the weakest suit in sight.
When dummy's on your left,
Lead through heft.

9) DUMMY SURROUND

When making a lead, the top of a sequence is normally the best you can do.

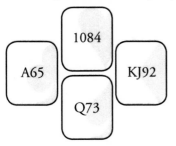

The underlined cards are the proper leads from these sequences. However, utilizing these sequences with the middle card missing is not going to occur to many. Basically, you borrow that card from dummy if it is on your right. Just as you borrow three points from partner when balancing, in this technique you are borrowing a card from the dummy.

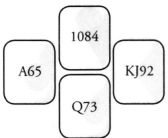

In this combination, if you were to lead the two, following the advice of yesteryear (fourth highest) Declarer could duck and eventually make his Queen. But notice the effect of you borrowing the 10 from dummy. You now have a three card sequence, so lead the Jack. But before you become too enamoured with this play, be aware that you have to have a higher card, in this case it is the King. This maintains your tenace which is an important technique that was highlighted earlier.

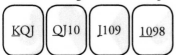

Now, let's examine this technique more closely. If you are the R.H.O. leading this suit, only one card will prevent Declarer taking a trick. Let's look at all of them in turn. If you lead the 2, Declarer ducks and eventually wins a trick with the Queen. If you lead the 9, same scenario. If you lead the King, careful play by Declarer will get him a trick. Only by leading the Jack can you stop Declarer from winning a trick. Notice that you have the J/9 surrounding dummy's 10. To capitalize on this holding, you must lead as if the 10 was yours and you were leading top of a sequence. Once again, notice the presence of the King in that same hand. There must be a higher card there so that it will still have a tenace over the 10. Maintaining a tenace if at all possible is not only basic to good Declarer play but can also apply to defence. Notice that moving a card over to partner's hand changes nothing.

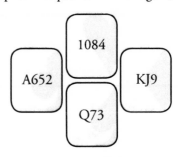

Here's one to try for yourself.

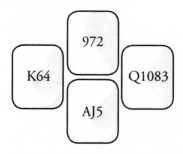

In the previous example, Declarer was held to no tricks because of the dummy surround play. In this last one, proper technique holds Declarer to the one trick to which he was entitled. You might want to lay out the cards and see if there is any lead and subsequent play, other than the 10, which might give Declarer a second trick.

Although this technique is more commonly used when surrounding the 9 and 10, surrounding the Jack can also be a winning strategy. By leading the Queen, R.H.O. maintains a tenace over dummy's Jack and although Declarer can win the King, a subsequent lead of the suit by L.H.O. gets the defence three tricks, in a N.T. contract.

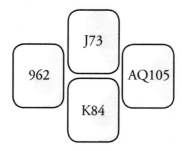

10) TOTAL TRUMP

This is better known as the *'Law of Total Tricks'*. The concept has been around for many years but had lost favour soon after its inception. It has more recently been championed by Larry Cohen. Although this law, in its entirety, is much more involved than the following, this basic explanation is sufficient for our purposes. In a competitive auction you are reasonably safe bidding to the level of total trump held by you and partner. In other words, holding a total of eight trump, you can bid for eight tricks and with 9 trump, you can bid to the three level. It is for this reason that I prefer to call it the *'Law of Total Trump'*. Not all hands are played at game or slam. Probably more than half of them are played in part scores. So the player who does well in part score skirmishes, whether declaring or defending will consistently come out on top, over the long hall. Here are some sample hands where applying this law guides you in your decision making.

"I forgot we were vulnerable!"

♠ A9653			
♥ QJ2			
♦ KJ5			
♣ Q7			

You	L.H.O.	Part.	R.H.O.
1♠	Dbl.	2♠	3♥

Should you bid 3♠?

Absolutely not! You have a minimum hand and partner has only promised three trump. You might have only eight trump in total. Partner will go on holding a fourth trump.

♠ Q962			
♥ J			
♦ K643			
♣ Q532			

You	L.H.O.	Part.	R.H.O.
P	P	1♠	2♥
2♠	3♥	P	P

Should you bid 3♠?

Absolutely! Partner, by passing is confirming only five trump. He expects you to go on if you have more than three.

♠ Q753
♥ K10
♦ K86
♣ Q952

Holding this hand, you hear partner open a weak 2. If it's Hearts, pass. If it's Spades, bid 4.

11) LOSING TRICK COUNT (LTC)

This method of determining the trick taking potential of a hand has been in existence for three generations. Many years after its inception, a revival took place in the sixties. However, it once again slipped to the back burner. And yet, when used as a companion of point count, after a trump fit has been established, it is extremely useful in judging how high to bid. It should be noted that the LTC does not replace the point count evaluating methods already in place. As mentioned above, it is an added tool used in the judgement process after a trump fit has been uncovered. Because of the method used to count losers – a loser exists if you have a missing Ace, King or Queen in any given suit – there can only be a maximum of three losers in any suit. Of course, a worthless singleton or doubleton would only be one or two respectively. Therefore, any hand of four suits can only have a maximum of 12 losers. Add partner's 12 to your own and yours and partner's hand will have 24 in total. And that is the essence of the LTC. You can usually, because of the partner's bids, estimate the number of losers in partner's hand, add them to yours and subtract the total from 24. The answer tells you how many tricks your side can reasonably expect to take. So, if you were to add this valuable tool to your bidding methods, you would soon realize the following:

- As points increase, losers decrease
- As points decrease, losers increase
- Unbalanced hands have fewer losers
- Balanced hands have more losers

In the case of balanced and unbalanced hands, the number of losers changes even if the different hands have identical H.C.P.

One other factor must be considered if planning to adopt the LTC. Just as adjustments are made when evaluating a hand using H.C.P., so it is when using the LTC. These adjustments can raise or lower the LTC depending on the quality of your points, as well as quality and number of trump held. Distributional values also have a bearing. Quality points are honours grouped in one or two suits. For example, A/K in the same suit will almost guarantee two tricks, but will K/K/J when spread across three suits. Yet, each is 7 H.C.P. When spot cards are in long suits, grouped with honours, they are much more valuable than doubleton or tripleton spot cards not accompanied by honours.

As well, keep in mind those seemingly insignificant 9's and 10's. Although they are not assigned any H.C.P., they act as bodyguards for your honours. In combination with honours, they are very valuable indeed. The Queen and Jack in an enemy suit are practically worthless. But add a 9 and/or 10 and see them grow in stature. So, as soon as one of you limits your hand, partner can estimate (quite accurately) your LTC, add it to his/hers and determine how many tricks those 26 cards will likely take. However, here's one of those always present caveats. Although the LTC is accurate in predicting the trick taking power of your two hands, it assumes that suits will break normally and that half of your finesses will be successful.

In the following table, the number of losers shown is the average number when using the LTC. You would then make your adjustments, up or down, taking the appropriate factors into account.

OPENING ONE OF A SUIT

Minimum (13 – 15)	7 Losers
Intermediate (16 – 18)	6 Losers
Maximum (19 – 21)	5 Losers

OPENING N.T.

Although the LTC only applies after a trump fit has surfaced, knowing what to expect from an N.T. opening is also helpful.

1 N.T. (15 – 17)	6 Losers
2 N.T. (20 – 21)	5 Losers
3 N.T. (28+)	3 Losers

OPENING PRE-EMPTS

Weak 2 (6 – 11)	8 Losers
Weak 3 (6 – 11)	7 Losers
Weak 4 (6 – 11)	6 Losers
Weak 5 (6 – 11)	5 Losers

"I have a count of 18... I think."

RESPONDING TO ONE OF A MINOR

Raising:

1♣ to 2♣	8 losers	*(5+ trump, no 4 card major)*
1♣ to 3♣	9 losers	*(5+ trump, no 4 card major)*
1♦ to 2♦	9 Losers	
2 N.T.	8 Losers	
3 N.T.	7 Losers	

RAISING ONE OF A MAJOR

2♥ or 2♠	9 losers *(3 trump)*
2 N.T.	7 losers *(4+ trump)*
3 N.T.	7 losers *(3 trump)*
3♣ *(Bergen)*	9 losers *(4+ trump)*
3♦ *(Bergen)*	8 losers *(4+ trump)*
3♥ or ♠	11 losers *(4+ trump)*
4♥ or 4♠	10 losers *(not Vul.)*
4♥ or 4♠	9 losers *(Vul.)*

1.

♠ KQ7632	♠ A1054
♥ AQJ	♥ K72
♦ AQ4	♦ K1086
♣ 5	♣ QJ6

1♠	2N.T.
3♦	4♦
4♥	5♥
6♠	

The bidding shown below these hands utilizes control bids to reach a laydown 6 ♠. The 2N.T. bid is Jacoby which announces game – going values with at least four trump in support of partner. Four ♦ shows second round control (K or Singleton). The same applies to each partner's Heart bids. With neither showing a Club control, only a small slam can be bid.

Using the L.T.C., the bidding would look like this:

1♠ - 2N.T. *(Jacoby)*

3♠ - 4♠ *(No Controls)*

4N.T. - 5♦ *(Blackwood & 1 Ace)*

6♠

Opener could have signed off in game after the 2N.T. bid. By bidding 3 ♠, opener is beginning the investigation for slam. With partner showing only one Ace, opener settles for 6 ♠. With opener having only four losers and responder showing eight [24 – (8+4) – 12] the slam was a laydown.

2.

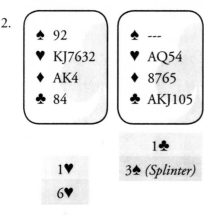

♠ 92
♥ KJ7632
♦ AK4
♣ 84

♠ ---
♥ AQ54
♦ 8765
♣ AKJ105

	1♣
1♥	3♠ *(Splinter)*
6♥	

In this hand, control bidding and/or Blackwood aren't even necessary to reach the unbeatable 6 ♥. The splinter bid announces 19 points which translates to five losers. Responder with seven losers can confidently bid six.

3.

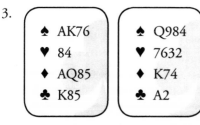

♠ AK76
♥ 84
♦ AQ85
♣ K85

♠ Q984
♥ 7632
♦ K74
♣ A2

Although L.T.C. applies only when a suit fit has been uncovered, N.T. bids will at least give a general idea of the number of losers. So, if a N.T. opening and responses such as Stayman or a Transfer lead to a suit, knowing how many losers to expect in opener's hand can be very valuable. A 1N.T. opening will be six losers at most. Following is just such a sequence, leading to a fit and with subsequent use of the L.T.C. to a game which would seldom be bid using more conventional methods. After a 1N.T. opening and a Stayman response leading to a Spade fit, responder, knowing that opener's hand had six losers was able to bid game holding eight of his own.

OPTIONS

Left to a Person's Discretion or Choice

Although Bridge, to newcomers, appears to be beset by hard and fast rules, nothing could be further from the truth. True, the game is ripe with clichés put forth by our mentors, but those who aspire to competent play must apply good judgement and common sense, above all else.

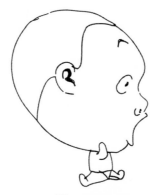

*"You mean you
opened on that!"*

1) Process Of Elimination

Although a process of elimination is very often the saving grace when contemplating a bid, it is none the less valuable in determining a course of action when declaring. In the following hand, how an adverse suit is breaking has a profound effect on the course Declarer must take.

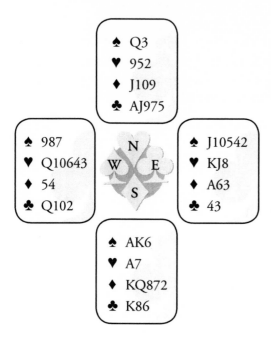

♠ Q3
♥ 952
♦ J109
♣ AJ975

♠ 987
♥ Q10643
♦ 54
♣ Q102

♠ J10542
♥ KJ8
♦ A63
♣ 43

♠ AK6
♥ A7
♦ KQ872
♣ K86

Contract: 3N.T.
Opening Lead: ♥4

The opening lead is most certainly fourth highest. The question, for Declarer, is whether it was from a four or five card suit. If it's a four baggar, then R.H.O. has four and all is well. If it's five, then attacking Diamonds in an effort to develop the additional tricks required, is an exercise in futility. The defence will then get their ♦ and 4 ♥ to defeat the contract.

Therefore, it is critical that Declarer watch the return of R.H.O. on trick two. If it's the 3, meaning an original holding of 4, Declarer can attack Diamonds with impunity. If it's a higher card, meaning that R.H.O. started with 3, Declarer should eliminate Diamonds from his plan and attack Clubs by finessing L.H.O. for the Queen. There is no guarantee that attacking Clubs would be successful but one hope is better than none.

Only Your Own Inherent Weakness of Purpose Will Defeat You

2) WHICH SUIT?

As a defender, which suit or suits to hang on to when discarding is often critical. There are many guidelines available to aid in this decision making because a defender cannot see Declarer's or partner's hand. Try not to discard from four card suits and keep length with dummy are but two. Declarer faces the same sort of problem when deciding which suit or suits to attack when he hasn't enough tricks to make the contract. So, in a N.T. contract, Declarer must look at the end result when contemplating which suit to attack. If the chosen plan will not produce the required number of tricks, Declarer must look elsewhere. The following hand is a case in point.

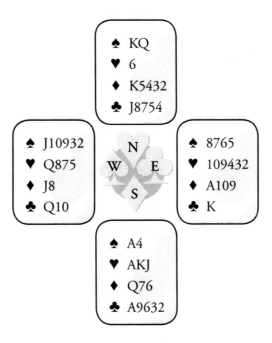

Contract: 3 N.T.   Opening Lead: ♠J

Before proceeding with the analysis of this hand, a basic defence against N.T. contracts should be addressed. In an auction such as 1N.T. – 3N.T. where neither a transfer or Stayman has been employed, attacking a major suit is the winning strategy more often than not. With just such an auction, L.H.O. chose to lead Spades although that might have been the lead in any case. Counting tricks, Declarer could see two ♠, two ♥ and at least four ♣ – only eight in total. Where would the 9th trick come from? Sometimes, when needing to solve a problem, Declarer can enlist the aid of the opponents.

Most defenders try to get some value for their Aces, so when Declarer won trick one in the dummy and led a low Diamond, R.H.O. opponent was reluctant to contribute his Ace and Declarer's Queen won the second trick. Having acquired a fortunate Diamond trick, that was all Declarer needed and proceeded with the Clubs to bring his total to nine tricks.

**"Is that bid supposed
to be psychic?"**

3) Don't Trump, Dump

According to the Encyclopedia of Bridge, a loser on loser play is the act of discarding a known loser in one suit on a loser in the suit being played. As shown in the Encyclopedia there are as many as ten reasons for employing this technique, one of which being the promotion of a trump trick for the defence. The following hand deals with just such a necessity.

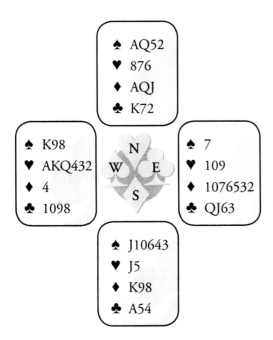

Contract: 4♠
Opening Lead: ♥A

One of the basics of good defensive play is to count your certain tricks and if that number is insufficient to defeat the contract try to envision a distribution of the cards which will permit defeat. And one such ploy is a trump promotion. However, just as Declarer must cash all the side winners before embarking on a cross-ruff, so must a defender cash all side winners before trying for a trump promotion. Therefore after cashing two top Hearts, L.H.O. realized that no more tricks were available in Hearts, his ♠King looked like a dead duck and prospects in the minors didn't look any better. So he tried for a trump promotion by leading a small Heart, hoping partner could trump high enough (an uppercut) to force Declarer to over ruff with an honour. But Declarer hadn't been asleep and exercised the countermeasure suggested by the above title. He dumped a loser (a ♣) instead of overtrumping.

The Road To Success Is Always Under Construction

4) DANGEROUS OPPONENT

A dangerous opponent is one who can run an established suit, lead through an unprotected honour, give his partner a ruff or continue a forcing defense. Any of these can spell disaster for Declarer. As a result, competent Declarers will employ any means available to keep the dangerous opponent off lead. These means take the form of avoidance plays.

Declarer will finesse through the danger hand, not into it or he will duck to avoid the danger hand getting the lead. The following hand will illustrate finessing through the danger hand, as well as showing Declarer choosing one option over another.

The Seeds Of Knowledge Are Cultivated By Experience

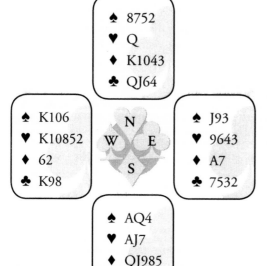

Contract: 3 N.T.
Opening Lead: ♥5

When a Declarer counts winners in an N.T. contract and comes up short of the total needed, the common practice is to immediately try and establish winners in the longest suit. Here that suit is Diamonds. But the second part of such a plan, and one which not enough Declarers utilize, is to project how the play will go. By doing so, in this hand, Declarer will realize that establishing Diamonds will only bring the trick total to seven but worse still is that it allows the dangerous opponent to get the lead and continue the Hearts through Declarer's A/J. This will establish Hearts for West and when the Club finesse loses, the Hearts will be cashed defeating the contract. Yet, if Declarer tries the Club finesse first – in a shorter suit – the contract is secure because West cannot continue Hearts from that side. Now when the Diamond lead loses to the Ace, Declarer is safe because he still has the Heart stopper. You have endplayed L.H.O. on trick #2. Brilliant!

The next hand shows Declarer using avoidance by ducking a trick to the non-dangerous opponent.

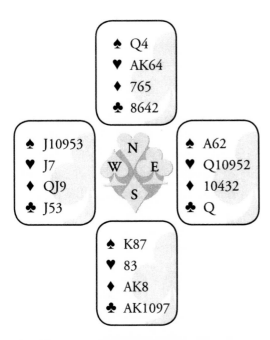

Contract: 3 N.T.
Opening Lead: ♠J

It should be obvious, having five tricks in ♠, ♥ and ♦, that the other four must come from ♣. However, the Spades could prove to be Declarer's undoing. As a result, not only must R.H.O. be kept off lead, but must also be exhausted of Spades so that if he did get the lead, getting to opener's hand would be impossible. To put this two-part plan into action, Declarer waited until the third trick to win his Spade then he crossed to dummy with a Heart and led a Club. When R.H.O. showed up with the Queen, Declarer simply ducked the trick. Mission accomplished, Mr. Phelps.

"This is what I warned you about."

5) Through Aces

Leading through Aces manifests itself in a number of ways. It could be a simple finesse such as this:

You simply lead a small card towards the King. If L.H.O. has the Ace and doesn't play it you'll make your King immediately. If L.H.O. plays it, you'll make your King on the next round of the suit. And if R.H.O. has it, you were never going to make your King against proper defence.

Leading through Aces is basic to an obligatory finesse. With this holding the only way to make three tricks is to lead through the hand which you suspect has the Ace. If you win that first trick with your King or Queen, next play a small card from both hands to the second trick. It might be your lucky day. The Ace may appear on that second rick without your having to play your other honour and you'll have your three tricks. Another way of leading through Aces is with combinations such as these:

By leading towards your double honours, you are hoping that one of those double honours wins the first trick. Then you return to the bottom combination in another suit and again lead towards the remaining honour of the original double honour. If the Ace is in the hand playing before the double honour and has to be played without capturing one of your honours, you'll make three of your honours. Here is a hand to illustrate.

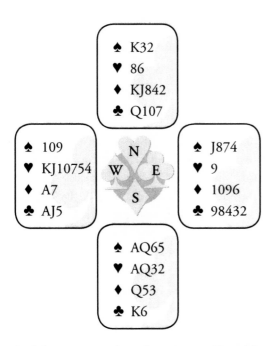

♠ K32
♥ 86
♦ KJ842
♣ Q107

♠ 109
♥ KJ10754
♦ A7
♣ AJ5

N
W E
S

♠ J874
♥ 9
♦ 1096
♣ 98432

♠ AQ65
♥ AQ32
♦ Q53
♣ K6

Contract: 3 N.T.
Opening Lead: ♥J

With L.H.O. having opened the bidding, it was obvious where all the missing points were located. Declarer took the opening lead with the Queen and immediately attacked Diamonds by leading a small card towards dummy. When the King held, Declarer returned to his hand with a Spade and again led a small Diamond. This time L.H.O. had to take his Ace and Declarer had his nine tricks – three ♠, two ♥ and four ♦.

6) FINESSES

Most players are familiar with the basic finesse and its different guises. As Oswald Jacoby said, a successful finesse is winning a trick with a card that is not the highest one still in play. Basic finesses are leading towards high cards, examples being A/Q, KX, etcetera.

 A basic finesse might also be a combination such as this, where you lead through the presumed Ace and then duck a second round. This is called the obligatory finesse. The following one is the backward finesse. By leading

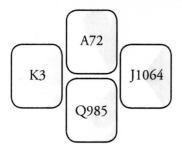 the Queen and having it covered, you win your Ace and then finesse against the ten. The most difficult finesse to visualize is the intra finesse. Lead the 9 and if it isn't covered, let it ride. Upon regaining the lead, cash the Ace, felling the King and then lead toward the Q8. Imagine missing KJ10 in a suit and losing only one trick.

The ruffing finesse is fairly straight forward but is not utilized by  nearly enough Bridge players. Faced with this card combination and needing an extra trick most would lead towards the high cards and if L.H.O. didn't cover they would insert the Jack, then bemoan their bad luck if the finesse lost. And these same players would take this type of finesse even if they knew the King was on the right. However, those familiar with the ruffing finesse would handle this card combination much more competently as illustrated by the next hand.

"A good peek is better than trying a finesse!"

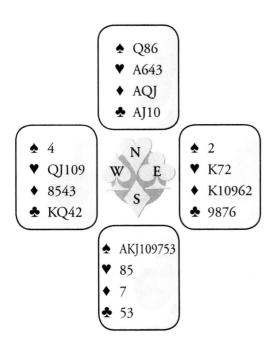

♠ Q86
♥ A643
♦ AQJ
♣ AJ10

♠ 4
♥ QJ109
♦ 8543
♣ KQ42

♠ 2
♥ K72
♦ K10962
♣ 9876

♠ AKJ109753
♥ 85
♦ 7
♣ 53

Contract: 6♠
Opening Lead: ♥Q

The unfortunate reality of some Declarer play techniques is this finesse isn't recognized by too many players. As an example, look at this hand. Most Declarers would take the opening lead, draw the opponents trump and lead a Diamond, finessing the Jack. That would be the normal finesse and would lead to defeat when R.H.O. cashed a Heart after winning the Diamond.

Yet look what happens when Declarer uses a ruffing finesse. At trick two, Declarer takes the ♦Ace and then leads the Queen. If R.H.O. covers, Declarer ruffs and later throws either a Heart or a Club loser on the established ♦Jack. If R.H.O. doesn't cover, Declarer immediately discards the remaining heart. And if L.H.O. wins the ♦King, Declarer has already shed a loser and will get rid of the other one on same established ♦Jack. The great advantage of a ruffing finesse is that you can discard two losers instead of one while maintaining control throughout the process.

Summing up the topic of finesses which present themselves in every hand, you might call them ubiquitous. The problem with finesses is that they are successful only 50% of the time. I've actually seen a regular partnership who rely solely on finesses as a plan. On a bad finesse day they'll usually finish hear the bottom and on a good one will look like the second coming of Goren himself. Many refer to such players as finessaholics and suggest that they join the 'F.A.' The 50/50 aspect is precisely why good Declarers will find other techniques to accomplish their goals and turning to a finesse only as a last resort. And this is also why the topic was ignored until others had been discussed. Don't be like the person on a seafood diet. They see food, they eat it. A finessaholic sees a finesse, he takes it.

*Play In Haste And
Repent At Leisure*

Although taking a finesse cannot be avoided in many cases, few Bridge players handle this ploy to best advantage. Finessing properly is really handling different card combinations properly. And because there are a great many combinations which Bridge players must learn to handle well, the suggestion here is to get a copy of this author's previous book called, *'Bridge: The 7 Deadly Sins'*. In it, as many as 100 different combinations are illustrated showing the best way to handle them from all sides of the table. In reality, *'Card Combinations'* are two of the 4 C's which make a good Bridge player. The other two are *'Concentration'* and *'Counting'*. Always remember the golden rule of finessing.

*Finesse Only If
You Must*

7) SWITCH SUITS

Breaking new suits, as most experienced players are aware, is very often a losing strategy as doing so will usually cost a trick or two for the side breaking the suit. Here are two examples.

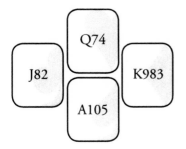

Here, whether Declarer or a defender is first to lead the suit the opponents will get two tricks and in the case of Declarer or dummy leading, possibly three tricks for the defence.

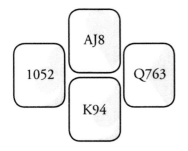

Here, switching to this suit by either defender costs a trick.

It is for this reason that most competent players are loathe to break new suits. A classic example of this philosophy is defending 1N.T. Although such a contract is difficult for Declarer, it is much more so for a defender. As a result, experienced players, when defending 1N.T., simply return the same suit whenever they win a trick. This is in keeping with the philosophy of not breaking new suits. They reason that they are giving Declarer tricks to which he was entitled rather than one to which he wasn't, which often occurs when a defender breaks a new suit. Although this philosophy is very often a winning strategy against 1N.T., it is much less successful against 3N.T. So, a defender shouldn't become so enamoured with the technique that he stops thinking. In the following hand, a 3N.T. contract, following this 1N.T. defending philosophy is tantamount to raising a white flag.

A Neglected Opportunity Seldom Returns

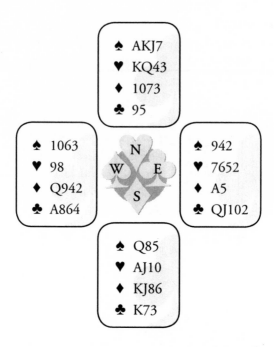

Contract: 3N.T.   Opening Lead: ♦2

With the opening lead being a Diamond, Declarer can easily make nine tricks if R.H.O. is one of those dogmatic players who belongs to the school which advocates the return of partner's suit at all costs. And in this case a return of partner's suit is a high cost indeed. But look what happens if R.H.O., upon winning that opening lead, switches to the Queen♣. The first five tricks belong to the defenders. This defender was a member of the school which advocates leading up to weakness. Remember the poem!

8) CHANGING SUITS

Although the definition of an option suggests that it is left to an individual's own discretion, there are many occasions where the individual really has no choice and must follow a certain course. And so it is in Bridge. By examining all the options, a Declarer might conclude that there is only one way to the promised land. The following hand illustrates just such a scenario.

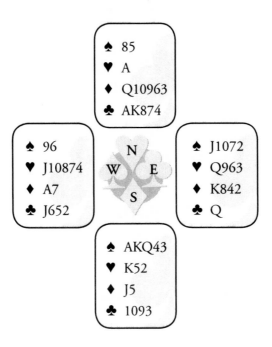

Contract: 3N.T.   Opening Lead: ♥J

Counting winners, Declarer has three ♠, two ♥ and two ♣ – two short of his goal. Two more could come from ♠ if they broke 3 – 3 but that is unlikely and putting all Declarer's eggs in that basket would be unwise. Trying Diamonds would be futile because by the time Declarer established two extra tricks in that suit, defenders would win the race with three ♥ and two ♦. All this analysis leaves Declarer with no choice but to attack Clubs. After winning the first trick in dummy, Declarer cashes a high Club and upon seeing East's Queen must unblock the suit by playing the 10 or 9.

Now a small Club is led from dummy towards the remaining high Club in Declarer's hand. Although this is contrary to the guideline of leading towards high cards, it does cater to the possibility that East started with Q/J or that

West started with four Clubs. If this second Club lead is taken by West, Declarer has two extra Club tricks and his contract. If West foolishly doesn't take the ♣Jack, it is now finessable for an overtrick.

Although breaking new suits often gives away a trick or two, there are times when it can be beneficial. This hand illustrates how Declarer can benefit form breaking a new suit. This same philosophy is demonstrated by the last hand in the previous section, titled '*Through Strength*'.

Failure Is Just An Opportunity To Begin Again

9) TRUMP ACE

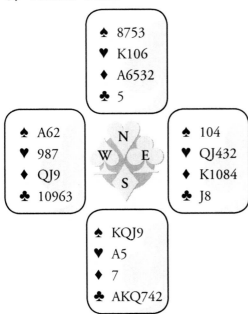

♠ 8753
♥ K106
♦ A6532
♣ 5

♠ A62
♥ 987
♦ QJ9
♣ 10963

N
W E
S

♠ 104
♥ QJ432
♦ K1084
♣ J8

♠ KQJ9
♥ A5
♦ 7
♣ AKQ742

Contract: 6♠
Opening Lead: ♦Q

A common guideline for a defender is to take countermeasures to Declarer's line of play. So, when Declarer tries to draw trump, many defenders with nothing else to guide them, will deliberately hold back their trump Ace. After all, if Declarer wants it played, they take the stance, "What am I, a puppet?" As a result, they are occasionally left holding the bag, so to speak.

If the Ace becomes the only outstanding trump, Declarer will often leave it out there. The defender holding that Ace ends up trumping with it and getting virtually nothing for such a valuable card. There are times when you might need to take the trump Ace quickly. For example to give partner a ruff while he still has some trump or to make a needed switch in suits, to name but two. However, as mentioned, if there is nothing else to guide said defender, the best time to take the trump Ace is when there is exactly one trump remaining with it. Then that last trump can be led for maximum effect. Applying that philosophy to this hand, it can be readily seen that taking the first trump lead will allow Declarer to establish Clubs for the slam-going tricks. If the Ace is taken when trump is led the second time and returning the last trump, a defender scuttles that plan. In this game of cat and mouse, called Bridge, the defender and Declarer are both following accepted wisdom – defender maximizing possession of the trump Ace while Declarer, after drawing one round of trump, sets about establishing a side suit before completing the drawing of trump.

LOOK OUT

*To Draw Attention to a Thing or Circumstance
that Constitutes a Peril*

As has been mentioned, over and over again, the greatest difficulty in bidding is knowing the true value of your hand and then passing on that knowledge to partner. This statement leads quite logically to the first four items that follow:

Four Things That Come Not Back:
The Spent Arrow
The Spoken Word
The Past Life
The Neglected Opportunity

1) BIDDING SAME VALUES

The problem that arises if a bidder doesn't know a hand's true value is that said bidder might bid the same values more than once. For example, each of the following hands can bid only once. Any subsequent bid would only occur if forced, by responder (partner) to do so. In each of these cases, your first bid has been on minimum values and bidding again with nothing from partner would be a losing strategy.

1. If L.H.O. overcalls and partner passes, don't bid again.

2. If L.H.O. passes your one ♦ opening and partner responds at the one level, your only rebid is 1N.T.

3. If L.H.O. overcalls your one ♣ with a ♦ bid, only a negative double should illicit a positive response from you.

4. If partner were to respond, at the two level, to your ♥ opening, your only rebid is a raise of the minor.

5. Raise a ♥ or ♦ response. Bid 2N.T. if it's a ♣.

Making any other rebid with these minimum opening hands would be committing the sin of bidding the same values twice. It's overbidding which gets most partnerships into difficulties.

Here's a hand where bidding the same values twice gave the opponents a second chance to bid a makeable game and they didn't let the second one go by.

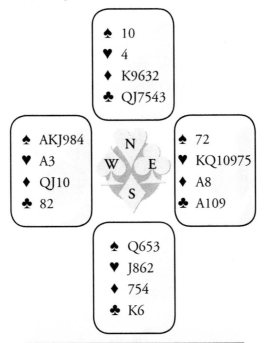

East	South	West	North
1♥	P	1♠	2N.T.
P	3♦	3♠	4♦
P	P	4♠	P

If allowed to play four ♦, N/S would likely be down three. Even doubled but not vulnerable would cost 500. A bad return on their investment when E/W might have been happy to play in a part score. By bidding again, North allowed the opponents to bid their makeable game in Spades. Even that, not vulnerable, would only have been 420. If E/W had been vulnerable their score would be 620 and the 500 would have been a net gain for N/S. However, the 4 ♦ bid would still have been too risky since it might have gone for 800 against best defence, vulnerable.

Failure Is Success If We Learn From It

2) Six/Five, Come Alive

As is a well known fact in Bridge, H.C.P. are quite accurate in projecting how many tricks can be taken in a N.T. contract when two reasonably balanced hands are opposite each other. However, when they are grossly unbalanced, H.C.P. take a backseat to the trick-taking power of a suit contract. Take note, those of you who simply can't bring themselves to open with less than 13 points or to bid game with less than 26. In the following hand, the H.C.P. are fairly evenly split and yet both sides can bid and make a small slam because of very distributional hands.

You Can't Build A Reputation On What You Are Going To Do

♠ QJ109
♥ 87642
♦ ---
♣ KQ96

♠ 8643
♥ KJ
♦ KQ52
♣ 753

N
W   E
S

♠ ---
♥ AQ1095
♦ A987643
♣ 4

♠ AK752
♥ 3
♦ J10
♣ AJ1082

The bidding:

East	South	West	North
1♦	1♠	2♦	3♣
3♥	4♣	4♦	4♠
5♥	6♣ or ♠	P	P
P			

One of those ubiquitous guidelines of Bridge is that, in a hand where the bidding continues unhesitatingly to a high level, it is obviously a very distributional hand and if you have any doubts about bidding, sweep them out of your mind and bid on. So, if South bids 6 ♣, East should bid 6 ♦ and if South bids 6 ♠, East should counter with 7 ♦. East can't be sure that 6 or 7 ♦ will make but it sure looks like N/S can make a small slam in either black suit and the slight penalty for going down in 7 ♦ wouldn't hurt a bit. Hence the title of this section. With a hand like East's you must get into the bidding and compete instead of sitting back waiting for the opening lead. Note also how East has bid the longer suit first and then bid and rebid the shorter. This is the correct way of bidding a hand which is 6/5 in its longest suits. The fact that it is actually 7/5 changes nothing and is simply icing on the cake.

3) Forcing Pass

Quite often, when your side has bid comfortably to a game, the opponents will sacrifice. They feel that any penalty which they incur will still be a net gain. In other words the points which you receive for defeating their contract will be less than you would gain by declaring and bringing in your own. When this happens, whether to bid on or let them declare, is often a difficult decision and better made by both of you. Enter the *'Forcing Pass'*. If your R.H.O. has obviously made such a bid and you are unsure of the best action which you could take, enlist partner's help. A pass in this situation says, "Partner, I'm unsure of whether to bid on or double. You decide." Partner is strongly urged to take one action or the other. A pass on partner's part is not an option. Here's a hand to illustrate.

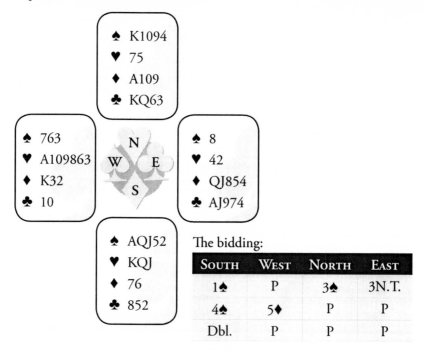

♠ K1094
♥ 75
♦ A109
♣ KQ63

♠ 763
♥ A109863
♦ K32
♣ 10

♠ 8
♥ 42
♦ QJ854
♣ AJ974

♠ AQJ52
♥ KQJ
♦ 76
♣ 852

The bidding:

SOUTH	WEST	NORTH	EAST
1♠	P	3♠	3N.T.
4♠	5♦	P	P
Dbl.	P	P	P

Fearing that N/S were heading for a makeable game in Spades, East began to prepare for a possible minor suit sacrifice by bidding 3N.T. This was the unusual N.T., showing at least 5/5 in the minors. When South did bid the Spade game, West felt justified in sacrificing at five ♦. West didn't know that South couldn't make four ♠, losing a ♥, a ♦ and two ♣. North couldn't be sure what action to take so he made a *'Forcing Pass'* and left the decision to partner. With North having made a limit raise, South was certain that bidding on would be foolish and being a member of both of the following schools – the five level belongs to the opponents and get the most you can from each hand – doubled for penalty. North, being a member of a third school – lead trump when they sacrifice – led the ♦Ace and followed it with a second trump. This eliminated two ♣ ruffs in Declarer's hand and two ♥ ruffs in dummy. The result was not pretty, down three. Had North made the more conventional lead of the fourth highest Spade, Declarer would have escaped with down one, or two depending on the defenders' skill.

*Well-Timed
Silence Can Be
More Eloquent
Than Speech*

The value of trump leads cannot be overstated. And when they sacrifice is a classic example of 'make them pay.'

4) LAZINESS

As a leading Bridge authority, now deceased, once said, "The average Bridge player makes 100 mistakes in a session of Bridge and is rarely aware of any more than 5." As a matter of fact, that statement is the basis of this author's third book. It's title, *'Bridge Faux Pas, Let Me Count The Ways.'* And the contributing characteristic which leads to these errors is laziness. Sadly, laziness at the Bridge table continues to be this author's major failing. The following two hands illustrate how defeat continues to be the product of this flaw in the average Bridge player's make-up. One shows Declarer falling victim and the other a defender.

Rules Of Success Don't Work Unless You Do

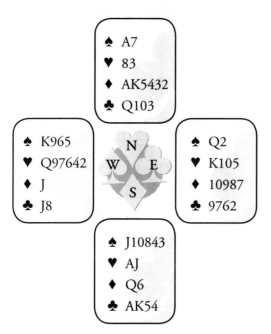

```
            ♠ A7
            ♥ 83
            ♦ AK5432
            ♣ Q103

♠ K965          N          ♠ Q2
♥ Q97642    W     E        ♥ K105
♦ J             S          ♦ 10987
♣ J8                       ♣ 9762

            ♠ J10843
            ♥ AJ
            ♦ Q6
            ♣ AK54
```

Contract: 3N.T.
Opening Lead: ♥6

Counting winners in this contract shows one ♠, one ♥, three ♦ and three ♣. Declare, feeling quite confident that the Diamonds would yield overtricks, quickly took the opening lead and began on the Diamonds – Queen first of course, he knew how to unblock suits. But when West showed out on the second Diamond, Declarer suddenly felt a little chill run through his bones. If he continued Diamonds in an effort to establish them, the defenders would rain Hearts and add a little dampness to his chill. Declarer had failed to consider that the Diamonds might break badly. Had he done so, he might have first looked at an alternate line – the Clubs. Sometimes, when missing six cards to the Jack, you must hope the Bridge gods are in your corner and play for the drop. Drop or even finesse for the Jack. Playing for the drop is the same principle as the handling of a doubleton honour.

<table>
<tr><td>KQxx
Jxx</td><td>To get three tricks from this suit, it is best to lead small towards the double honour. If L.H.O. is forced to play the Ace (he holds Ax) without capturing one of your honours, you'll have three tricks. In</td></tr>
</table>

today's hand, a thinking Declarer will investigate the Clubs firstly before placing all his eggs in the Diamond basket. That would produce four ♣ tricks and total nine even if the Diamonds broke badly. And if they did break normally, there would be 12 in all.

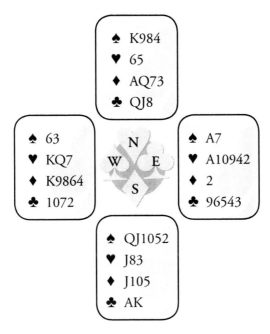

Contract: 4♠   Opening Lead: ♥K

In this hand, a slumbering defender missed a golden opportunity to defeat the contract. East knew from partner's lead of the King that he also had the Queen. Instead of using the nine to signal for a continuation of Hearts, he should have overtaken the opening lead and led his Singleton Diamond. Then, when Declarer went after the trump, he could have taken the trump Ace, led a Heart to partner's Queen and received a Diamond ruff to set the contract.

Noah Didn't Build the Arc In The Rain

5) WHAT CAN GO WRONG?

As is obvious, Declarer has quite an advantage over defenders since he can see all his assets while defenders can see only their own hands and dummy. However, just as a defender can lose the advantage of the opening lead by a thoughtless one, so can Declarer lose his inherent advantage by not giving enough thought to the play before proceeding at trick one. If all looks rosy after counting winners and losers, Declarer should adopt a pessimistic view and ask himself the above question. And, if he doesn't like the answer to that question, he should take the necessary precautions. In the following hand, the finessaholic would definitely go wrong.

What We Look For, Often Determines What We See

"How was I supposed to know?"

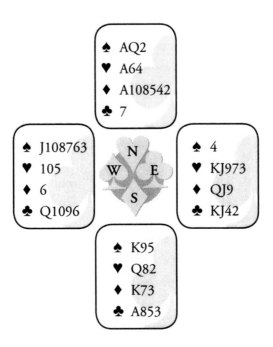

Contract: 3 N.T.   Opening Lead: ♥10

The opening lead was a natural with partner having overcalled Hearts during the auction. A basic requirement of Declarer and partner of the opening leader is to interpret the opening lead. Doing so is very revealing a high percentage of the time and not doing so, by Declarer, can prove disastrous. The bidding and opening lead very strongly suggest that East has the ♥King and that Declarer has the Queen.

Although holding up with such a Heart holding is normal, it is normal only when a switch would not be damaging. With these forewarnings, Declarer should take the opening lead in dummy and immediately begin Diamonds. This approach would guarantee ten tricks. And if Declarer couldn't resist trying to win trick one with his Queen – once a finessaholic always a finessaholic – East having interpreted the lead should see the futility of continuing Hearts and look for a profitable switch. A switch to Clubs wouldn't be long in coming and suddenly Declarer would be wishing that he could replay the first trick.

"I thought we were playing Diamonds"

6) GETTING WINNERS TRUMPED

As was pointed out in the previous section, a good Declarer always visualizes the source of the tricks necessary to fulfill the contract. And then said Declarer takes the necessary precautions to protect those contract fulfilling tricks.

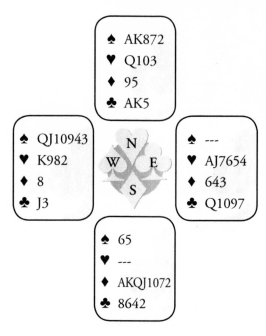

♠ AK872
♥ Q103
♦ 95
♣ AK5

♠ QJ10943
♥ K982
♦ 8
♣ J3

♠ ---
♥ AJ7654
♦ 643
♣ Q1097

♠ 65
♥ ---
♦ AKQJ1072
♣ 8642

Contract: 5♦
Opening Lead: ♠Q

West's opening 2 ♠ bid sounded the alarm for Declarer. However, he wasn't listening. It shouldn't have been too difficult to conclude, from the opening bid, that East was void of Spades. But Declarer covered the opening lead, had it trumped and couldn't recover.

Counting winners, Declarer could count two ♠, two ♣ and seven ♦ for 11 in total.

All he had to do was make sure one of those Spade or Club winners wasn't trumped and all would be well. By ducking the first two Spades, he could have trumped a continuation of Spades and after drawing trump could have discarded his Club losers on dummy's A/K of Spades. The following ancient proverb, when heeded, is worth a bucket of master points.

Millions Of People Cannot Hear, Many More Will Not Listen

7) GETTING OVERRUFFED

One of the many basics to good Declarer play is to count your losers as soon as dummy hits the table. If there are too many, a good Declarer looks for ways in which some or all of those losers can be eliminated. As already mentioned, if all appears to be in order, Declarer asks "What can go wrong?"

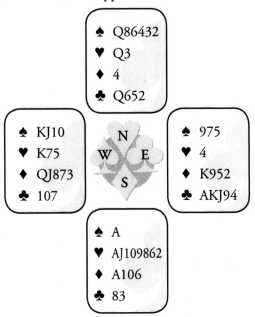

♠ Q86432
♥ Q3
♦ 4
♣ Q652

♠ KJ10
♥ K75
♦ QJ873
♣ 107

♠ 975
♥ 4
♦ K952
♣ AKJ94

♠ A
♥ AJ109862
♦ A106
♣ 83

And if there is something which can go wrong, our hero takes the necessary precautions. In this four Heart contract, the bug in the balm would be getting overruffed on the third trick. A second basic of good Declarer play is to count the tricks which are going to fulfill your contract. L.H.O. leads the ♣10 against 4 ♥ and after taking two tricks R.H.O. continues with a high Club. If Declarer ruffs this trick, it gets overruffed and then L.H.O. returns a trump to cut down on Diamond ruffs in dummy. Declarer, having chosen this line of play eventually finishes down one. However, if Declarer ruffs the third Club with the Ace of trump, planning to ruff two Diamonds in dummy, his only losers are the two ♣ and the trump King. It pays to count where your game going tricks are. In this hand, Declarer avoided an overruff by trumping high. In the following hand, Declarer avoids the overruff by ducking and severing the communications between defenders.

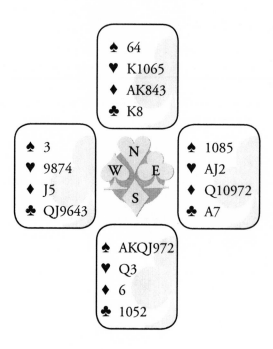

Contract: 4♠   Opening Lead: ♣Q

Because West is not likely underleading the Ace, covering the Queen will accomplish nothing. However, ducking might be very beneficial. But, when faced with a situation where a duck could be employed, Declarer must always consider what might happen if that defender might make a more devastating switch when allowed to hold that first trick. In this case there is no disastrous switch available to defender. So, let's look at how the play might go if Declarer covers or doesn't cover the opening lead. If the Queen is covered, East will win and likely return a Club. West will win and lead a third round which will be ruffed in dummy and overruffed by east. With the Heart Ace still to be lost, Declarer will be down one. However, if it isn't covered, this effectively scuttles communications between the defenders and the overruff situation never arises.

What Happens Next Is The Critical Time After A Mistake

8) Leading Or Underleading Unsupported Aces

The number of times that this grievous error on opening leads is committed is of epidemic proportions. Well, I suppose such a statement is a bit of a stretch but none the less, it is done far too often even by the more experienced players. In their defence of such a heinous crime, they offer, "I wanted to see the dummy so that I could decide what to do next." Unfortunately, in most cases, the damage has already been done and recovery is beyond reach. Having done so, they've made Declarer's King into a trick. Had they waited for partner to lead the suit, that King would have been a dead duck. Worse still, is setting up both the King and Queen for Declarer. And absolutely devastating to the defence is underleading the Ace, losing that trick to a Singleton King and having the Ace trumped, possibly setting up multiple honours for Declarer. A leading Bridge authority even refuses to lead an unsupported Ace in partner's suit, attacking elsewhere just to avoid doing so. Viewing a complete hand or two is unnecessary to illustrate the folly of this crime against humanity. Here are some isolated suits to demonstrate such foolishness.

1.

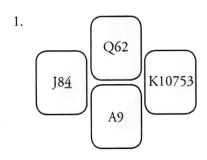

When partner leads the four – low from an honour – you can be sure it's the Jack because he wouldn't have underled the Ace. Therefore, you can safely play your 10 if dummy plays low. It will force the Ace and now dummy's Queen is trapped. Had you not been able to trust partner's lead, you might have played your King on the first trick, making dummy's Queen into a winner. Although it should be admitted that good defenders would likely have held onto the King to protect against the Queen. However, change the 10 into an 8 and third hand might have played the King, following the advice that third hand should at least be able to contribute the 9.

Even more devastating to the defence, when an Ace is underled is the breakdown in partnership harmony and trust. There is no better example of how underleading an Ace, when partner believes you don't do such unthinkable things, than the following.

2.

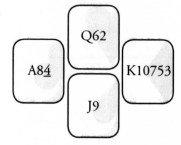

When the 4 is led, partner, believing the lead to be from the Jack, will play the 10. What if the Jack had been a Singleton? Because L.H.O. had broken this suit, dummy would make the Queen. This is a trick which materialized because a defender had broken a new suit. Better to have led something else.

♠ A1064
♥ 762
♦ A83
♣ A95

In the following example, a complete hand, not wanting to underlead an Ace, a defender must lead trump. As unpalatable as this is to many, leading trump in today's game is not the lunacy it was thought to be in yesteryear. Hearts are trump. Leading a Heart is much more logical than underleading an Ace. According to today's accepted wisdom, leading trump won't necessarily gain a trump trick whereas underleading an Ace might well cost one. If you can't strike a positive blow for the defence, the least you can do is take a neutral stance rather than a negative one.

"Just don't do it."

9) LEADING OR UNDERLEADING UNSUPPORTED KINGS

There are very few times when leading an unsupported King is a winning strategy. However, two instances where doing so would be wise are when holding a Doubleton King (Kx) in partner's suit and if your analysis suggests that it is the only way to gain the necessary tricks needed to defeat Declarer.

As pointed out in the previous section, leading an unsupported Ace is too often a poor decision. However, many players will do so if their holding is a Doubleton (Ax). Their hope is that they would be able to ruff the third round. Such a scenario doesn't usually occur because partner has to gain the lead at some point to give them that ruff and they have to have some trump left when he does. Yet there is no guarantee that both of these requirements will be met. These players continue to make these leads because they remember that it worked once, way back when. They conveniently forget the many times that it cost them a trick or more.

The same occurs too often with Kings. These same players think such a lead (Kx) will produce a ruff on the third round. However, it seldom does for the same reasons that leading from Ax is seldom successful. And in the case of the King, had it not been led or underled, it might have been a winner later.

However, as mentioned, if that unsupported King could be led as a faint hope, do it. After analysing the situation and determining that leading the unsupported King is the only road to success, then it is the correct thing to do.

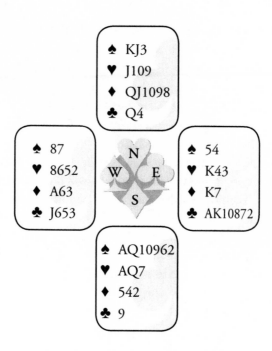

Contract: 4♠   Opening Lead: ♣3

After taking the first trick, East began surveying the landscape. Where could the defence possibly collect four tricks? Since all the Kings were in sight and Declarer had 13 points about the only card of value which partner might hold would be an Ace. Surely Declarer had the trump Ace. If partner had the ♥Ace, it would mean only two tricks in addition to the opening Club. East therefore led the ♦King at trick two. When it held he continued to partner's Ace and received a ruff to defeat the contract. Notice that East did not try to cash a second Club before leading the Diamond. He had reasoned that the opening lead had been fourth highest from an honour, making Declarer's nine, a Singleton. Thinking always triumphs over dogma.

10) BLOCKING & UNBLOCKING

This has happened to all Bridge players, even those who are now world class calibre. It can happen to Declarer as well as defenders, although far less frequently to Declarer because he can see all his assets. This is precisely why Declarers have been taught to play the high card from the short side first when running a long suit. However, this is easier said than done when defending. Blocking a suit simply means not being able to cash the remaining cards in a suit because you can't get to them. The solution to this dilemma, in the following hand, is very difficult to spot. However, once it is recognized, the simplicity is truly remarkable.

Things Alter Spontaneously For The Worse, Unless They Are Deliberately Altered For The Better

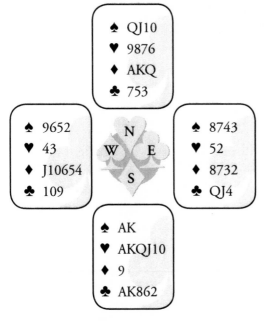

The bidding of this hand is of no consequence. Some hands are difficult to bid even when they have been dealt normally. This hand, having been constructed to illustrate a point, really doesn't need an explanation of the bidding. The opening Diamond lead in this 7N.T. contract has put Declarer in dummy for the first and last time.

There doesn't seem to be any play for 13 tricks because only two Spade tricks are available. However, by discarding the A/K of Spades on dummy's Diamond winners and then discarding the three small Clubs from his hand on dummy's Spades, 13 tricks are there for the taking.

The preceding hand is a dramatic example of Declarer unblocking a suit. In the following examples, we see defenders making what seem to be foolish plays just to get out of partner's way.

Although this can happen to Declarer as well, it is a crime committed, most often, by defenders.

Following to partner's suit or in returning partner's suit, you must get out of partner's way. This is precisely why advice such as the following has long been the standard. When returning partner's suit, play the highest if your original holding was 3. By doing so the suit will likely never be blocked with partner holding established cards which he cannot cash. However, a more dramatic unblocking occurs in these three examples.

1.

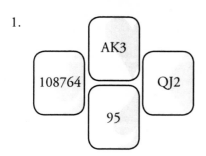

Partner leads the 6 against 3 N.T. It should be obvious that he is leading fourth highest from a four or five card suit, headed by the 10. So, when dummy plays the Ace, you must begin the unblocking process by dropping your Queen and when the King is played, you must let go of your Jack.

2.

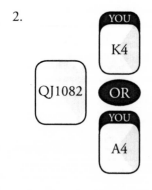

Partner leads the Queen, top of a sequence. You must play your King or Ace on that first trick so that you'll have a low one to return to partner. In the case of the Ace, you've set up Declarer's King. No matter, he was entitled to it anyway and you've at least cooperated with partner in the establishment of his suit. And if Declarer's King was a Singleton, you look like a genius.

3.

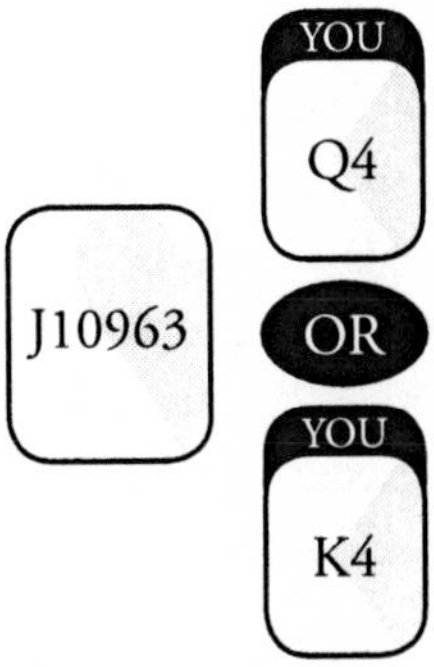

YOU

Q4

J10963   OR

YOU

K4

An identical situation calls for identical treatment. When partner leads the Jack, get out of the way quickly, drop your honour.

11) BATH COUP

This not difficult technique is being mentioned here rather than with other

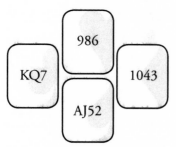

Coups simply because, as a defender, you should be on the look out for it. And since a complete hand is not really necessary to illustrate, here it is. You lead the King and it is allowed to win. If you continue the suit, you've handed Declarer two tricks. Mind partner's signals. By playing the 3, his lowest card, partner is denying interest in a continuation. However, a crafty Declarer might contribute the 5 to that first trick, leaving the impression that your partner was beginning a 3/2 attitude signal. A countermeasure against such a Declarer is find another opponent. Playing against such people is no fun at all.

Actually, there is a defensive countermeasure against such a Declarer ploy. It is called the *'Bath Coup Buster'* and will be addressed with the other coups.

The Bath Coup Is Not Beating Your Roommate To The Tub

12) DISCARDS

"Parting is such sweet sorrow." I'll bet that you didn't realize that this statement originated in the Bridge world. However, making a discard is quite often just plainly painful. Yet, discards can be far less painful and much more productive if some of the guidelines which have been in existence for years are used as just that – guidelines. The following list, although not complete, does highlight the most common of these guidelines. They are presented in groups where there are similarities and a basic explanation is given for each. It should be noted that following the advice given in each will not always be possible because of the particular circumstances which exist at the time a discard must be made. However, an effort must be made to follow the guideline if at all possible.

Having To Do With Length

1. **Keep Length With Dummy:**
    Here's an example. Dummy holds AKQ4 in a given suit. Your holding is 9632. Notice that your highest card is better than dummy's lowest (9 over the 4). As soon as you discard from this suit, you've made the 4 into a trick.

When Asked About Your Discarding Methods, Tell Your Opponents That You Play 'Advil' Discards, Yours Give Partner A Headache

2. **Four Card Suits:**
    Because you can't see Declarer's hand, keeping length with Declarer is obviously more difficult. This is why experienced defenders try not to discard from 4 card suits.

3. **Partner's Long Suit:**

   Once you become aware of a long suit in partner's hand, either partner has led it initially or you've been counting, discarding from that suit is safer. However, keeping one, so that you would be able to lead it later is often a winning strategy.

4. **From Length Not Shortness:**

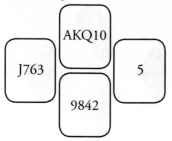

Discarding from length such as a five card suit is much safer than discarding from shortness. Not only do you run the risk of losing a valuable card, discarding from a short suit often exposes partner's holding. In this example, if you have discarded the 5 earlier and can't follow to the first lead of this suit when Declarer leads the Ace, partner's Jack becomes worthless.

Honour Sequences

1. **Unblocking:**

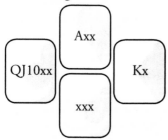

Defenders must always be aware of the need to get out of partner's way. For example, although there are other unblocking situations, consider the case of partner leading the top of a sequence against a N.T. contract. When partner leads the Queen and dummy plays the Ace, drop your King. This isn't a discard in the strict sense of the word but you might say that you've discarded an impediment.

2. **Top of a Sequence:**

   This is truly a discard and a dramatic one at that. And it is best appreciated by viewing a complete hand.

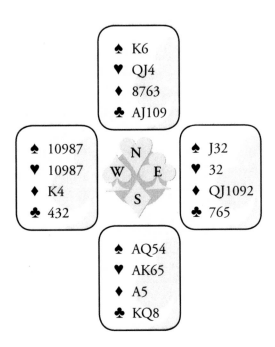

Contract: 7 N.T.   Opening Lead: ♥10

As Declarer cashes all four ♥ tricks, East must make two discards. By first discarding the ♦Queen, he is telling partner that he has a solid four card sequence in Diamonds, headed by the Queen. As a result, partner can discard a Diamond when Declarer cashes 4 ♣. Although this leaves the ♦King unprotected, no matter, partner has the Diamonds covered.

Notice that discarding a Spade from that West hand gives Declarer four ♠ and the contract. Although blanking the ♦King is something all players would be loathe to do, it is perfectly safe because of partner's dramatic discard of the ♦Queen.

Worthless Hand

Too often, with a worthless hand, a defender tends to get careless when making discards. In other words, discarding here, there and everywhere. All this defender is thinking about is the next hand. And yet, if this defender were to give his discards a little more thought, he would quickly realize that his discards can be very helpful to partner. Stripping a suit from his hand, although normally doing so is unwise because it is too revealing to Declarer, can aid partner in counting the hand.

Negative Not Positive

Most players will discard a high card in the suit which they want partner to lead. However, if you can't afford to part with a high card in that suit, better to discard a small (discouraging) card in a suit where you have no interest.

Conventional Discards

1. **Lavinthal:**
   If playing Lavinthal discards, your first discard denies interest in the suit which you are discarding. The size of the card indicates which one of the other two suits you want partner to lead. Here is a partial hand to illustrate.

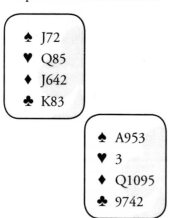

   On an auction of 1♥ - 2♥ - 4♥, partner leads a trump. Declarer wins and continues trump. Partner takes this second trump and you must discard. Discard a Club which asks partner not to lead a Club but to lead a Spade or a Diamond. If you want a Spade, discard the ♣nine. If you want a Diamond lead, discard the ♣two. A high discard asks for the higher ranking suit while a low discard asks for the lower.

2. **Odd/Even:**
   Using this method of discarding, an odd numbered card (3 – 5 – 7 – 9) encourages partner to lead that particular suit while an

even numbered one (2 – 4 – 6 – 8) denies interest. However, it seems to me that players when first introduced to this discarding signal might find it easier to remember if even was encouraging (E/E) But if you were to play it this way and were asked about your discarding methods you might have to say *'Reverse Odd/ Even'*, quite a mouthful.

3. **Partner's Suit:**
   If you discard all your cards in partner's suit, you are showing no outside entries. If partner starts discarding from his own suit, don't bother returning it.

**"Don't you have any
Spades at all?"**

BORN OF NECESSITY

Necessity Is The Mother Of Invention
To Recognize The Inevitable

As the title suggests, the headings in this section highlight those areas of thought which must prevail if success is to be achieved. And although many of these thoughts must be applied in each hand whether declaring or defending, there are inherent slight differences. Those referring to Declarer play appear first. Defender play follows and those which must be addressed from both sides of the table close out this section.

Many of the techniques outlined are closely associated with each other and will appear together as much as possible.

1) READ THE LEAD

Bridge teachers and writers have always emphasized the importance of the opening lead. They stress that choosing the suit to lead is determined, to a great degree, by the bidding and then by the mode – aggressive or passive – which the leader wishes to adopt. However, once the suit decision has been made, the card which is led from that suit is governed by convention. Remember *BOSTON*.

Bottom

Of

Something

Top

Of

Nothing

Basically, this acronym is saying that you lead a small card to indicate values at the top of the suit. Conversely, if you lead a high spot card, you are denying possession of anything higher. Although this guideline covers many leading situations, there are others to consider. For example, leading a high honour in a side suit would be either the top of a sequence or top of touching honours. While leading a Doubleton honour in a side suit is frowned upon, it is the accepted wisdom in partner's suit. And of course, a high spot card led could be the top of a Doubleton while any card can be a Singleton. With all this information, about opening leads to guide them, the opening leader's partner and Declarer should begin placing the missing cards in that suit.

In the following exercise, the opening lead is given. As leader's partner, you should know within reason what opener holds in the suit led. First, a side suit. Try to make your determination before looking to the explanation of each.

1.	Ace	Leader has the King and at least one other card. Maybe even the Queen.
2.	King	Leader has the Queen. He might also have the Jack or ten or both.
3.	Queen	Leader has the Jack. He might also have the 10 or 9 or both.
4.	Jack	Leader has the 10. He might also have the 9 or 8 or both. Maybe the King.
5.	Ten	Leader has the 9. He might also have the 8 or 7 or both. Maybe the Queen or King.

In all above cases, the leader is promising the card below the one lead. Opener might also have the third card down, making it a solid sequence. If opener has the fourth card but is missing the third, it is a broken sequence. Notice that Declarer is denying possession of the card above the one led but might have the next card up when leading the Jack or 10. This would be leading from an interior sequence. Whichever of these sequence leads has been made, it is always the top of touching honours.

Notice that there has been no reference to an honour lead in a side suit being the top of a Doubleton against a suit contract. Players doing so are hoping to get a ruff. However, such a ruff seldom materializes since it is necessary for partner to obtain the lead while the leader of the Doubleton still has trump. Both of these scenarios seldom develop, making such a lead a losing strategy more often than not. And while we're on the topic of honour leads, you might want to add 'Jack Denies' and '10 Implies' to your defensive strategies. This statement simply means that leading a Jack denies possession of a higher card, while leading the 10 implies that you have one or two non-touching higher cards.

However, if you adopt the 'Jack Denies, 10 Implies' strategy, you have to give up other combinations, such as also holding the King or Ace above the Jack.

Another reason for not leading Doubleton honours in side suits, especially Kings or Queens is that Declarer might finesse the wrong way and you have a chance of making that honour, while leading it is tantamount to giving it away. Now to continue reading those opening leads.

6.	Nine	Leader has nothing higher. It might be top of nothing or top of a Doubleton. Although this type of Doubleton lead seldom bears fruit just like Doubleton honours.
7.	Eight	Is also likely to be top of nothing.
8.	Seven	Could be top of nothing but could also be third or fourth highest from one or two non-touching honours.
9.		Any card led which is lower than the seven is most likely third or fourth highest from one or two non-touching honours.

Having trust in partner's leads is paramount. Knowing what they are likely to be and then examining dummy and your own hand enables you to have a pretty good handle on Declarer's holding in the suit which partner has led. And don't forget, if the lead is a low spot, to apply the *'Rule of 11*'*. As far as leading partner's suit is concerned, let's start by dispelling one of the rules held over from Whist. **Don't** lead the top card in partner's suit as a matter of course. Leads in partner's suit should be the same as in other suits except, as already noted, that leading the honour from the Doubleton is the accepted wisdom.

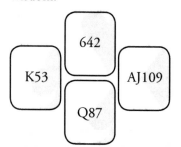

Here is an example where leading the top of partner's suit proves to be costly. If you lead the 3, as you would in a side suit, Declarer gets no tricks.

If you lead the King, advice from the days of Whist, Declarer gets a trick with the Queen.

*For those who don't fully understand how this rule works, here is a more detailed explanation. By assigning numerical values to the honours in a suit, the Jack would be 11, the Queen 12, the King 13 and the Ace 14. In a line, they would look like this.

The Will To Prepare Is More Important Than The Will to Succeed

									J	Q	K	A	13 cards
2	3	4	5	6	7	8	9	10	11	12	13	14	in all

If a player's lead is fourth best, that player has three cards on the scale which are higher than the one led. For example, let's say the opening lead is the 5. It, as well as the three higher cards, held by the opening leader, have been highlighted. That leaves precisely six cards, higher than the one led, in the other three hands. If the opening lead is fourth best, this mathematical calculation cannot fail. $(11 - 5 = 6)$ When the application of the rule gives a strange answer, the lead was not fourth highest. If it would seem to be third highest, apply the *'Rule of 12'* and if fifth highest, apply the *'Rule of 10'*.

									J	Q	K	A	
2	3	4	5	6	7	8	9	10	11	12	13	14	

In this third highest lead, the leader has two cards higher than the 6, so the others at the table have a total of 6. $(12 - 6 = 6)$

									J	Q	K	A	
2	3	4	5	6	7	8	9	10	11	12	13	14	

Here, using the *'Rule of 10'* with a fifth highest lead $(10 - 3 = 7)$ the others have seven cards higher.

Here's a simple way to remember these three rules.

1. **Rule of 10:**

   $10 + 5 = 15$ When a lead is fifth highest, you subtract the card from 10 to calculate the number of cards, which are higher than the one led, held by the other three hands.

2. **Rule of 11:**

   $11 + 4 = 15$ Subtracting the value of the card from 11, when the lead is fourth highest, announces how many higher cards are in the other three hands.

3. Rule of 12:

12 + 3 = 15   If the card led is third highest, subtracting its value from 12 reveals the number of cards which are higher, in the other three hands.

With each of these rules, whatever the lead may be, 3rd, 4th or 5th highest plus the number of the rule will always total 15. No, this is not cribbage. For example:

3rd	Highest + Rule of 12 = 15
4th	Highest + Rule of 11 = 15
5th	Highest + Rule of 10 = 15

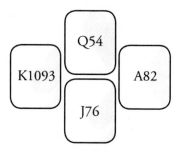

Q54

K1093   A82

J76

At this point, let's interject a little humour. This is the type of play which columnist Steve Becker might attribute to his fictitious 'Sylvia', everybody's nemesis at the local Club. She had her own unique way of playing the game and seldom received the bad result which she so richly deserved. Since one strange play deserves another she led the nine on the opening lead, Declarer played the Queen from dummy which lost to the Ace. Declarer's Jack was then a sitting duck under the King/10. A good defender would lead the 10 from this holding and a good Declarer would duck (mandatory) in dummy. This is precisely why it is difficult to play against inexperienced players. It is very difficult to read their hands.

Following is a summary of the preceding considerations as well as other guidelines which you could use in drawing conclusions.

1. As Declarer, if you are missing the King and Jack, when the opening lead is made play the lead to be from the King. If you are missing the Queen and 10, the lead is most likely from the Queen.

2. If the opening lead, in a suit contract, is not in the suit which defenders have bid and supported, it is very likely a Singleton.

3. If the opening lead would seem to be a foolish one, the leader probably felt another one would have been even worse. Guess who likely holds that missing honour that you are worried about.

What We See Depends On What We Look For

2) ENGINEERING A RUFF

A basic way for Declarer to eliminate losers is to trump them in dummy. However, that is often easier said than done. A case in point is mirrored suits. It's difficult to trump a loser if you have to follow suit. A mirrored suit is one which has the same number of cards in it on both sides of the table. Following is a hand which illustrates how to trump a loser in a mirrored suit – first break the mirror.

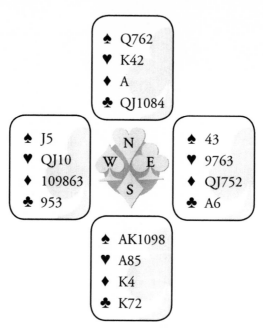

Contract: 6♠   Opening Lead: ♥Q

Counting losers shows one ♥ and one ♣. However, another basic way for Declarer to eliminate losers is to discard them on extra winners. If that extra winner is in the dummy, all is well. Declarer simply discards his loser – mission accomplished. But if that extra winner is in Declarer's hand, eliminating that loser becomes a two stage process.

To exercise that two stage process, in this hand, Declarer wins the opening lead in dummy and draws trump. The drawing of trump is often a necessary first step. On other occasions it can be left until other tasks have been completed and then there are times when drawing trump is delayed through necessity. The ♦Ace is then cashed and Declarer's hand is entered with the ♥Ace. On the ♦King a Heart is discarded from dummy and Declarer has successfully engineered a Heart ruff in dummy.

3) Dummy Reversal

Bridge is a game with so many guidelines and exceptions that standard occurrences are a welcome site. Two such standards which you could almost always take to the bank are that Declarer's hand will have the higher point total, as well as the greater number of trump in a suit contract. Dummy will only occasionally have more of either or both. It is for these reasons that a Declarer, when planning a line of play, will count losers in his hand, trump them in dummy then draw the defenders' trump with those in his hand. An example of dummy having more trump, when play begins, is after a transfer. On occasion both might start out with mirrored trump suits (same number on both sides), and by trumping a time or two in Declarer's hand, dummy becomes the long hand (more trump). These are situations which develop as a matter of course. But when it is done deliberately, dummy becomes Declarer and Declarer's hand becomes the dummy. In effect, the hand is played backwards. This is done because there is no other way to make the contract. Here's a sample hand showing a dummy reversal.

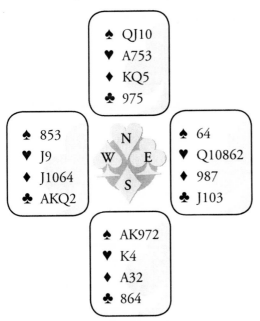

♠ QJ10
♥ A753
♦ KQ5
♣ 975

♠ 853
♥ J9
♦ J1064
♣ AKQ2

♠ 64
♥ Q10862
♦ 987
♣ J103

♠ AK972
♥ K4
♦ A32
♣ 864

Contract: 4♠
Opening Lead: ♣Ace

Things look rosy for Declarer. The only losers would appear to be the first three ♣. There are no trump losers. Two ♥ losers can be trumped in Declarer's hand and there are no ♦ losers. If you see the potential danger in this plan, go to the head

More failure stems from the fear of making a mistake.

of the class. If you haven't gone to the head of the class and need an explanation, here it is. You must trump dummy's Heart losers with the Ace and King of trump, returning to dummy each time by leading a small trump. In effect, dummy's Q/J/10 of trump extract those held be defenders.

4) Suit Establishment & Entries

As most experienced Bridge players are aware, successful techniques are almost always interwoven. And so it is with this combination of suit establishment and entries. There isn't much point in developing one of dummy's suits for discards if you will be unable to reach it. As has already been pointed out, ruffing in dummy and discarding on extra winners are two of the basic techniques for eliminating losers. So is suit establishment. But it is often overlooked by newer and experienced players alike. Following is a hand to illustrate this technique.

The Will To Succeed Goes Hand In hand With The Will To Prepare

Since developing a side suit for discards is influenced greatly by the division of the missing cards, let's first examine a basic premise which is utilized by most experienced players. Most refer to it as the '*Odd/Even*' rule. When the opponents have an even number of cards they are likely to divide unevenly more often than not. And if they have an odd number, those cards are likely to divide as close to evenly as possible.

CARDS MISSING	LIKELY DIVISION
8	5 – 3
7	4 – 3
6	4 – 2
5	3 – 2
4	2 – 2
3	2 – 1
2	1 – 1
1	1 – 0

Remember: When a card is singleton, play for the drop.

The following hand will not only point out the wisdom of establishing a suit for discards but also illustrate how to choose between two suits. This second point shouldn't be too difficult having just seen a chart depicting likely divisions.

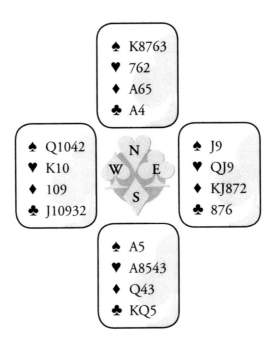

Contract: 3 N.T. Opening Lead: ♣J

Counting winners, as is the norm in N.T. contracts, shows two ♠ Spades, one ♥, one ♦ and three ♣ – seven in all. Two more tricks need to be established but the question is which suit to attack. Since there are two honours in Spades, many players would try Spades without giving it any further thought. Yet Spades will only produce one additional trick and two are needed. But look at the Hearts.

Although this suit drops from the Ace to the 8♥, there are eight cards in it, one more than in Spades. With Spades breaking 4 – 2 and Hearts 3 – 2, both as expected, attacking Hearts produces two extra tricks – mission accomplished. A good rule of thumb – if you have two suits which you might establish for extra tricks, pick the one where there are an odd number of cards missing rather than a suit where there are an even number.

In the following hand, again an example of establishing tricks, there is a trump suit which permits the trumping of losers to accomplish the task whereas in N.T. tricks have to be conceded to develop the extra tricks needed. It also illustrates the difficulty of playing hands where suits are mirrored — same number of cards in a suit on both sides of the table. Both Hearts and Clubs are mirrored suits.

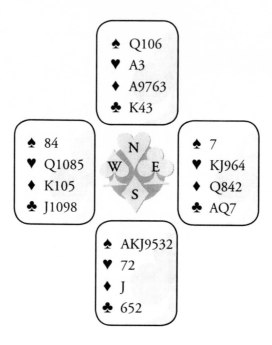

Contract: 4♠   Opening Lead: ♣J

After cashing three Club tricks, the defence exits with a Diamond. Having lost three ♣ and looking at a seemingly inevitable ♥ loser, Declarer has to put on a thinking cap. Whoever thought of mirrored suits should be penalized three tricks. With the trumping of losers or discarding them on extra winners not yet possible, Declarer had to look elsewhere.

Fortunately the possibility of suit establishment occurred to him. That technique, as mentioned earlier, doesn't occur to enough Declarers. However there had to be sufficient entries to dummy to establish the Diamonds and then be able to get to them once they were. Anticipating a 4 – 3 division – the norm according to the 'Odd/Even' rule of thumb – Declarer set about his task. With two Spades and the red Aces as entries, that wouldn't be a problem.

Declarer took the Diamond and ruffed a second one, entered dummy with a space and ruffed a second Diamond. He then crossed to dummy with another Spade and ruffed a third Diamond. This established dummy's last Diamond as a winner. So Declarer simply entered dummy with the ♥Ace and discarded his Heart loser on dummy's last Diamond.

5) END PLAYS

This is supposedly another one of those exotic techniques which only experts can execute. Nothing could be further from the truth. Just as the *'Bath Coup'* is simple to execute, so it is with the end play. The difficulty arises in recognizing the need to employ it and having the necessary resources. As already mentioned, ruffing in dummy and discarding on extra winners are probably numbers one and two on a list of priorities for Declarer play techniques. If these two techniques are unavailable, usually because of mirrored suits, competent Declarers will go to plan 'C' or beyond to accomplish their goals. Plan 'C' is suit establishment with the fourth priority possibly being the end play. At this point, it might be appropriate to mention another Declarer technique which might also minimize the use of finesses. Although some of these techniques are interchangeable, the finesse should definitely be a last resort – the other being a squeeze. Now back to end plays. Although this might be more easily understood by using the term *'Elimination and Throw-In'* or *'Strip and Throw-In'*, end play seems to have won out as the naming of this technique. And it does occur, most often, towards the end of a hand. The words *'Strip'* and *'Elimination'* are very appropriate because Declarer has stripped opponents of safe exit cards which can be led when thrown into the lead. When a defender, who has been given a trick, has no safe cards with which to exit he must make a lead which is favourable to Declarer. This example shows how a defender is end played.

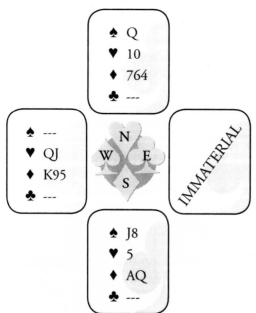

Eight tricks have already been played, with Declarer on lead. Spades are trump.

Declarer needs four of these last five tricks to make his small slam. Too many players would rely on the finesse, losing two of five instead of winning four. Holy finessaholic, Batman. By leading a Heart, Declarer throws the lead to L.H.O. who has no choice but to lead up to Declarer's tenace or give a ruff and sluff. As mentioned, it is the recognition of need and having the wherewithal which permits a Declarer to avoid a finesse.

Here is the complete hand, showing how Declarer has steered the play to this conclusion from the very beginning. It also shows the absolute necessity of reading the opening lead and retaining the knowledge gained.

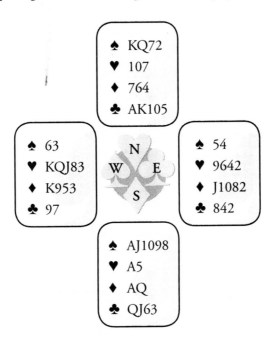

Contract: 6♠   Opening Lead: ♥K

Because of the opening lead, Declarer places West with the ♥Queen. Counting losers, reveals one ♥ and possibly a ♦. The Diamond finesse would lose only if the King was in the wrong hand. And, of course, it always is when a writer is trying to make a point. Having interpreted the opening lead, counted losers and not wanting to place all his eggs in one basket, Declarer embarked on his chosen course – an end play.

Basically, an end play strips two suits, throws a defender on lead with a third and thusly forces a favourable lead of the fourth or gives Declarer a ruff and sluff.

Leading either is really a Hobson's choice for the defender. In this hand,

Declarer wins the opening lead and draws trump – stripping one suit from defenders. He then cashes all his Clubs – stripping a second suit. At this point defenders have no black cards – they've been stripped of both. Now Declarer draws one more round of trump, forcing a further discard from defenders. This leaves a trump in dummy and two in Declarers hand, thereby retaining the ruff and sluff option should it be necessary.

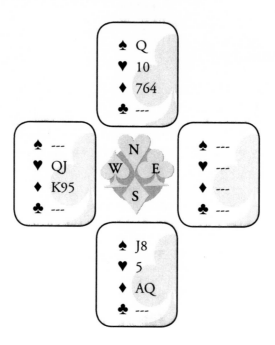

The diagram now shows the five cards remaining in each hand. Declarer leads his last Heart and the slam comes rolling home. Upon winning the Heart West can lead his last Heart, allowing Declarer to trump in dummy while discarding the ♦Queen. If West, instead, leads a Diamond it gives Declarer a free finesse.

6) SQUEEZES

For those who think *'End Plays'* are beyond them, the mention of a squeeze illicits complete bewilderment. Nonetheless, a squeeze is such an integral part of Declarer play that adding squeezes to one's Declarer play technique is a must if improvement is the goal. Here are the pre-requisites for a squeeze to be feasible.

1. Declarer, after counting losers and/or winners must be within one trick of his goal. In other words, if Declarer needs 12 tricks he must already have 11. If he needs ten, he must have nine and so on. If he is two tricks short, he must concede one of those losers as soon as possible. This is known in Bridge lingo as correcting or rectifying the count.

2. Declarer must have a card, which could become a winner in two different suits, depending on the play of a defender. These are called *'Threat Cards'*.

3. One defender has to have the burden of keeping a guard in both of those suits. These are called *'Busy Cards'*. Cards with which a defender can part, without dire consequences, are called *'Idle Cards'*. This is why the count had to be rectified. If it hadn't been, the hapless defender who had to protect his holding in two suits wouldn't have been so hapless. He would have had an idle card to discard when the moment of truth – possibly parting with a guard – had arrived.

4. Declarer must be able to reach the hand with a threat card or two. This is precisely the same problem that rears its ugly head when establishing a suit for discards – entries.

5. Declarer must first cash all winners in non-threat suits. Non-threat suits are suits where no more tricks are available regardless of how the defenders handle their cards in that suit. It's the cashing of the last card in a non-threat suit that applies the pressure to a defender who is trying to protect two guards, ultimately forcing him to part with one of them. In playing a suit contract, Declarer must not make the very common mistake of hanging on to his last trump as a safety measure. The last trump or the 13th card in another suit is what puts said defender

to his Hobson's choice. That last trump or 13ᵗʰ card in any other
suit is called the *squeeze card.*

Although there are many types of squeezes, the preceding information and
the following hand illustrate a simple type. Actually seeing a squeeze in
action will help to relieve the reader's anxiety and make more sense out of the
preceding verbiage.

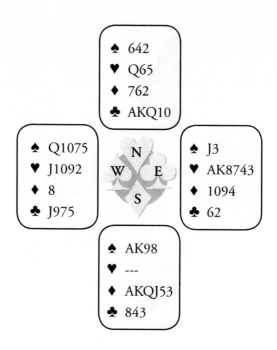

♠ 642
♥ Q65
♦ 762
♣ AKQ10

♠ Q1075
♥ J1092
♦ 8
♣ J975

♠ J3
♥ AK8743
♦ 1094
♣ 62

♠ AK98
♥ ---
♦ AKQJ53
♣ 843

Contract: 6♦   Opening Lead: ♥J

Taking stock, Declarer realized that he had to rely on a squeeze as no other
techniques seemed feasible. After trumping the first trick, Declarer rectified
the count by giving up a Spade trick. This meant that he was now within
one trick of the number he needed. In other words, he needed all of the
remaining 11 tricks but could only count 10.

When West won this Spade, he led another Heart, which Declarer trumped.
Declarer now led out his remaining four trump. On the first three, West was
able to play his trump and the last two Hearts. When Declarer led his last
trump this was the position. East's hand is immaterial and not shown. Poor
West was in trouble.

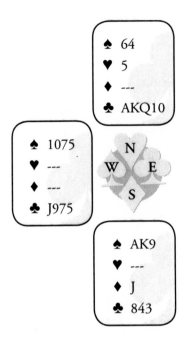

♠ 64
♥ 5
♦ ---
♣ AKQ10

♠ 1075
♥ ---
♦ ---
♣ J975

N
W E
S

♠ AK9
♥ ---
♦ J
♣ 843

If he discarded a Spade, Declarer could discard any one of the dummy's four losers with the other three going on his three remaining Spades. If West discarded a Club, Declarer would again discard a loser from the dummy, cash the Ace and King of Spades and discard his low Clubs and Spade on dummy's four Club winners. All of the prerequisites for a successful squeeze were implemented in this hand.

1. Declarer rectified the count by giving up a Spade trick.

2. Declarer's two threat cards were the ♣10 and ♠9.

3. L.H.O. had to protect both threat suits, Clubs and Spades.

4. Declarer had easy entries to both hands and threat cards.

5. Declarer cashed the non-threat suit winners first, trump.

And this is the essence of a successful squeeze. Make sure all the prerequisites are in place and then simply follow the prescribed course.

Now, let's look at the workings of a successful squeeze in a N.T. contract.

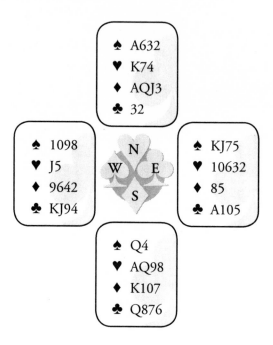

Contract: 3N.T.   Opening Lead: ♣4

The eagle-eye observer might have noticed that all four hands are 4 – 4 – 3 – 2. This distribution is the most common to occur when 13 cards are dealt to four players. So, it's not all that strange to see it in all four hands at once. Because the opening lead resulted in the defence taking the first four tricks, one of the requirements for a successful squeeze was realized immediately.

Declarer had eight of the nine remaining tricks – just one short of his goal. Although finding the Hearts split 3/3 would allow Declarer to make his 9th trick with the 13th Heart, he dismissed that possibility because a 3/3 split occurs only once in three chances and Declarer had a better idea. He could win the Spade led to trick five with dummy's Ace, thereby establishing a defender's King and then squeeze it out of him if that defender also had to protect Hearts.

Declarer might not have known the exotic name applied to this maneuver – the Vienna Coup. It will be examined more completely in the section on coups. With the first two requirements having been met and Declarer having two threat cards – in Spades and Hearts – that was the third.

Now, all Declarer had to do was cash fourth ♦ tricks and watch the pain on East's face. To this point R.H.O. (East) had discarded a Diamond on the fourth Club and followed suit to partner's Spade lead on trick number five. So, when Declarer cashed the four ♦ poor R.H.O. had to find three discards. He could safely discard two Spades but then what? All poor East had left was the ♠King and four ♥. Discarding from either suit would be fatal.

7) NEUTRALIZING A SUIT

This one will seem foolhardy to the uninitiated; holding up when having two stoppers in the suit attacked by the opponents.

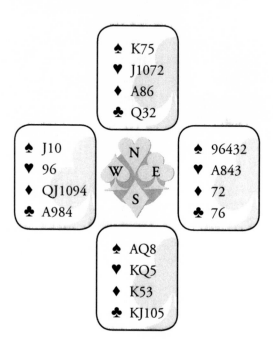

Contract: 3N.T.   Opening Lead: ♦Q

Counting winners reveals three ♠ and two ♦. To develop four more tricks requires that both of the round Aces be given up. As long as those Aces are not in the hand of the opening leader, there would seem to be no problem. However, if Declarer were to win the first trick and then try one of those rounded suits, his second Diamond stopper would be removed quickly.

When Declarer then attacked the other key suit, the defenders would take their remaining Diamonds and the contracts would be one down. By holding up on the first trick, Declarer effectively neutralized the defender's Diamonds. Here's the rule. If you have two key cards to dislodge from defender's hands (♣Ace and ♥Ace) and you have two stoppers in the suit which has been opened, hold up on the first trick. Simple, isn't it?

The preceding hand was an example of Declarer neutralizing a defender's long suit. In the following hand, a defender neutralizes a suit in dummy.

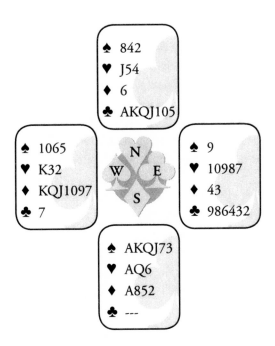

Contract: 6♠   Opening Lead: ♦King

No matter how Declarer attacked his problem of winning 12 tricks, there was no escaping reality – those Clubs in dummy had to be utilized – but how? There was no apparent entry. Eventually, Declarer saw a glimmer of light. Maybe, a defender would accept a gift. So, Declarer led the ♥Queen.

If L.H.O. had played the King, Declarer would have had his entry to those Clubs which would have provided a parking place for his remaining Heart and three Diamond losers. However, said L.H.O. smelled a rat or a Trojan horse and held-up his King. Notice that if Declarer had ruffed a Diamond to reach the Clubs, he couldn't have cashed enough of them to discard all of his losers – L.H.O. would have ruffed the second Club. And if Declarer had drawn all the trump before trying the Hearts, there would have been no trump in dummy to handle a Diamond continuation. Declarer's only hope was the Trojan horse but West's 'mama hadn't raised no fool!'

8) Finesses

Different types of finesses were discussed, with the ruffing variety in more detail, back in the *'Options'* section. Here we are going to examine finesses from a negative standpoint. Those players who take finesses wherever and whenever they appear will seldom give any thought to what might happen if the finesse were to lose. And this is why taking or shunning a finesse is an option which shouldn't be exercised without much prior thought. This basic principle is of the greatest importance when contemplating a finesse.

Although there are other reasons for avoiding a finesse, we'll deal here with only two – one where a losing finesse results in a ruff and the second where it allows the dangerous opponent to gain the lead.

A Peek Is Worth 1,000 Finesses Or Is It?

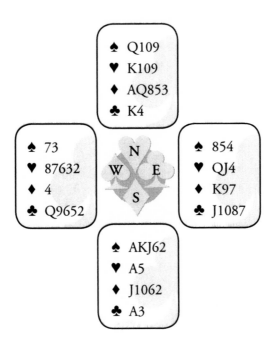

Contract: 6♠   Opening Lead: ♦4

With North having bid Diamonds, it is very likely that West is leading a Singleton. It can't be a Doubleton because the only two lower cards are the 3 and 2, which are both visible to Declarer. Being certain that it was a Singleton, Declarer rose with the Ace, drew trump and conceded a Diamond to bring in the small slam.

Taking that first round finesse is for finessaholics. Doing so would jeopardize the contract for the sake of an overtrick. The only time it would make even a modicum of sense is in duplicate and then only if there was a possibility that the lead was not a Singleton.

In the following hand, the R.H.O. is definitely the dangerous one and must be kept off lead at all costs. And the best way to appreciate the importance of doing so is to see a complete hand where Declarer has a two-way finesse for a missing Queen.

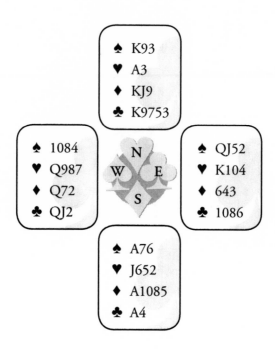

Contract: 3 N.T.   Opening Lead: ♥7

Counting winners reveals seven tricks in all – two short. Those two can easily come from Diamonds with a successful finesse. However, once Declarer has lost his lone Heart stopper, he must be careful to keep his R.H.O. off lead. Following is a technique which goes a long way towards the solving of two-way finesses.

9) TEMPT-A-COVER

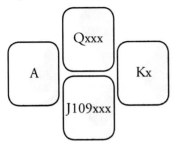

Qxxx

A

Kx

J109xxx

There's the story of a thinking Declarer who made a small slam missing the Ace, King and a spot in trump. He played Tempt-A-Cover and pulled off this swindle. He led the Queen from dummy, R.H.O. covered and you wouldn't have wanted to hear the post-mortem. We mortals can only perpetrate minor coups of this sort.

In the following layout you have a two-way finesse for a missing Queen. If you have no way of knowing which opponent has the Queen or how many cards each opponent has, play either the 10 or Jack, tempting second hand to cover – most live by the myth of covering an honour with an honour. If it isn't covered, second hand likely doesn't have the damsel. In that case win the trick on the opposite side and finesse for the Queen coming back. However, you must have the nine. You can work out, for yourself, what the scenario might be if you don't. This technique is reminiscent of the backward finesse. You lead the Queen. If L.H.O. covers, you win the Ace and finesse for the ten on the way back.

AJ93
K1074

Axx
QJ9x

10) R.T.T. (Retain The Tenace)

This topic very logically follows *'Tempt-A-Cover'* because both require two-way tenaces. The simplest definition of a tenace is to consider a three card sequence with the middle card missing.

As has been mentioned, a good Declarer will always look for pitfalls, especially when all looks rosy. With the following card combinations retaining the tenace is an absolute necessity to get as many tricks as possible from the suit.

1.

Q94
AK10762

If the missing four cards are split 3 – 1 or 2 – 2, there will be no problem bringing in the whole suit. However, if all four are in one hand, the situation requires a little more care. By cashing the Ace or King first, you'll still have the resources to finesse against the Jack if all four are in the same hand.

2.

Q862
AK953

If all four missing cards are on the left you can't avoid losing a trick in this suit. However, if they're all on the right you must cash the Queen first and maintain the AK9 over the J107.

3.

A93
KQ10654

If either defender has all four missing cards, cashing the King or Queen first allows for a finesse against either one.

In the preceding examples, a tenace was present on both sides of the table. In the following, a tenace only exists on one side. The correct technique in these is to play the winner or winners first from the side opposite the tenace. Notice that in each case, nothing can be done about all or most of the missing cards being in the hand which plays after the tenace.

1.

K9632
AJ854

Cash the King. If all three missing cards are on the right, they can be picked up by a finesse.

2.

AQ72
K1054

Cash the Ace and Queen first. If L.H.O. shows out on the second round, a finesse can pick up the Jack.

3.

KQ73
A962

Cash the King and Queen. If R.H.O. started with the Jack or 10 and three spots, this line of play will permit you to win all the tricks.

11) MAINTAIN COMMUNICATION

There is nothing more frustrating than to have winners in one hand or the other and not be able to get to them. This is precisely why a good Declarer watches entries like a hawk and a good defender unblocks. As a Declarer, employing techniques such as *'High Card From The Short Side First'* and *'Hold-Up'*, to name but two are winning strategies while defenders will normally make conventional leads and use signalling methods to maximize their trick taking.

In Any Human Endeavour, Communication Is Critical

"I had a lovely time."

The following hand will illustrate each of these techniques.

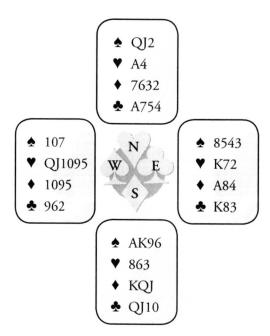

♠ QJ2	
♥ A4	
♦ 7632	
♣ A754	

♠ 107	♠ 8543
♥ QJ1095	♥ K72
♦ 1095	♦ A84
♣ 962	♣ K83

♠ AK96	
♥ 863	
♦ KQJ	
♣ QJ10	

Contract: 3 N.T.
Opening Lead: ♥Q

Notice how the card played from each hand is according to accepted technique with each side trying to maximize its trick taking. The opening lead is top of a solid sequence. Declarer holds-up the Ace in dummy and R.H.O. plays the encouraging 7. L.H.O. continues with the Jack and Declarer plays dummy's Ace (wishing he could hold-up for one more round).

R.H.O. now does his part by dropping his ♥King under the Ace. Declarer can no longer make the contract because of this unblock. Had R.H.O. held onto the ♥King there would have been no entry to those Hearts in partner's hand.

After taking trick two, Declarer will run the Spades by cashing the Queen and Jack in dummy (high cards from the short side first) and then leading to the Ace and King. However, Declarer needs four more tricks which could be available in Clubs but only with a successful finesse. And how many times have you seen that happen when the writer is trying to make a point. Notice that dislodging the ♦Ace would also lead to failure, again because of that unblock. However, a good Declarer wouldn't try the Diamonds anyway because that suit would only yield three tricks at best – not enough. So there you have it – perfect technique by both sides – one side succeeding with the other going empty-handed. Declarer did everything right but still failed. Life can be so unfair.

12) SIGNALS

Signals are to defence what flour is to baking. Without them defenders are playing with one eye closed. However, as a defender you must be ever vigilant. There is no reason to give a signal if partner isn't paying attention.

Many People Are Blind, But Many More Refuse To See

Sometimes these signals arise during the bidding. For example, if partner bids during the auction, you have a pretty good indicator of what suit you should be leading. Another example is the double of an artificial bid. When 2 Clubs by your R.H.O. is a Stayman inquiry, your double is requesting a Club lead. Similarly if a bid of Diamonds or Hearts is a transfer after a N.T. opening or overcall, double asks for the lead of the suit bid. A response to Blackwood doubled, is a lead-directing double.

Now to signals during the play. There are three types – attitude, count and suit-preference.

Drink at the fountain of knowledge, don't just sip.

Attitude

This is usually the first signal to appear during play. It is also the first one learned by beginners and often the only one. By playing a higher card than necessary when following to a trick led by partner, or when discarding, you are showing interest. Playing a small card shows no interest. Here are some examples:

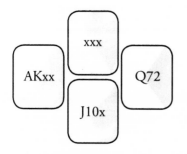

xxx

AKxx   Q72

J10x

When partner leads the Ace, promising the King, you play the 7 showing interest in a continuation. Partner has no way of knowing whether you could win the third round with the Queen or by ruffing but will dutifully continue with the King.

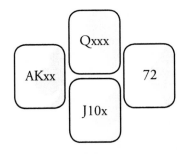

On it you'll play your 2 and partner will lead a third round. If the distribution had been as follows, you would have played your 7 and 2 in the same order and then been able to trump round three.

If your Doubleton was the Q2 rather than the 72 you would not play the Queen to show a Doubleton. Not only is that a waste of a high card but playing the Queen has a special meaning. Either you could win the second trick because the Queen was Singleton or with the Jack which your play of the Queen has promised. If asking for a special suit by discarding you should hold an Ace, Ace/King or the King behind dummy's A/Q. In the old days, playing high/low was called an echo. If you had no interest in a continuation because your holding looked like this 852, you would play the 2 first. Before we leave attitude signals, be aware that your interest or denial is not a command. Partner might have a perfectly legitimate reason for continuing or discontinuing the suit, regardless of your signal.

Signals Are The Legal Tender Of The Defence

Count

As is the case with most signals, experienced players widen the parameters of each. However, the basic count signal is best understood by examining a hand like the following:

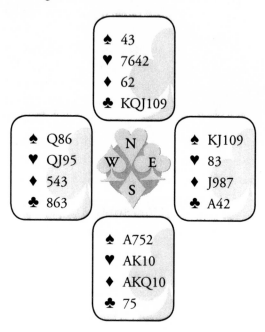

Contract: 3N.T.   Opening Lead: ♥Q

Having opened 2N.T., all at the table could be reasonably certain that South had a balanced hand and unlikely to have a long runnable suit. Having made that assumption, the defenders didn't need any help in taking their thinking one step further and realizing that Declarer had to score at least some of the Clubs to make his contract.

West realized that, if Declarer had Ace and another Club, the defenders' cause was lost. However, if his partner had the Ace there was hope for the defence but East had to know precisely when to take his presumed Ace. If he took it too soon, Declarer might still be able to reach dummy's nice suit. If he waited too long, Declarer might already have enough tricks from that suit to abandon it entirely.

Enter the count signal, stage left. Knowing that his partner would have a problem as soon as Declarer led a Club toward dummy, West played the three, a low card, indicating that he held an odd number. A higher card played first would indicate an even number. High/low says even. Low first says odd. Because the three was obviously West's lowest card (east had the two) this meant that East could take the second Club led and thereby eliminate dummy's Clubs. If West had played a high card first, indicating an even number, East would have known that Declarer had three Clubs and would have taken the third lead of Clubs. Depending on how many tricks Declarer had outside of Clubs, two Club tricks might have brought his total to nine. However, using the count signal would certainly have prevented overtricks.

Success Comes In 'Cans', Failure in 'Can'ts'

Suit Preference

This is the third way in which defenders can use signals when trying to get the best out of their cards. And as mentioned earlier, experienced partnerships are able to widen the parameters for this one as well. However, to simplify matters for those trying this signal for the first time or until you get comfortable with it, use it only when giving partner a ruff. And what better way to see this signal than through a complete hand.

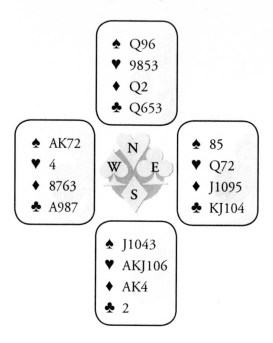

Contract: 3♥
Opening Lead: ♠Ace

Left to his own devices, Declarer would have no trouble bringing in nine tricks – five trump, a ♠ and three ♦. However, if the defenders are using attitude and suit-preference signals they can take the first five tricks. East plays the 8 on the opening lead and follows with the 5 when partner cashes the King. West now leads the ♠2 for East to ruff.

The two is significant because it is a suit-preference signal asking for a Club return. If he had wanted a Diamond led back he would have played the 7. A high card led for partner to ruff asks for the return of the higher ranking of the other two suits (excluding trump and the suit being led). A low card led asks for the lower ranking. Since West had the ♣Ace, he wanted a Club lead so he could give partner a second ruff. As a result of using signals, E/W were able to upset Declarer's apple cart. Without them defence becomes a guessing game.

13) TAKE CONTROL

It has been said that a revoke is just as much the fault of the revoker's partner as it is that of the one who commits it. After all you can prevent partner's revoke by simply calling attention to it. And there are many other ways in which partner's can help each other to prevent errors. Not only should they be formulating a plan as soon as dummy comes down but they should also be looking for ways to help in the decision making process. For example, if one partner has a clear picture of the defence needed, he should take control and not leave partner in the dark.

Quite often, from the opening lead, which could be crucial in itself to a point in the play where a special decision is required, only one of the defenders knows precisely what is needed to maximize the defense. When that moment arrives, 'he who knows, goes.' The following hands are classic examples of one defender taking control. He knew, so he went.

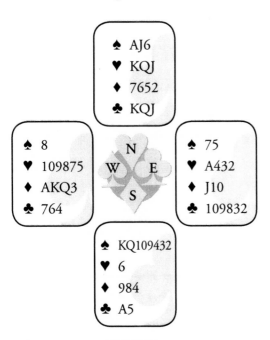

Contract: 4♠

Opening Lead: ♦A

West started with the top three Diamonds, noting partner's play of the Jack followed by the 10. On the third Diamond East had a problem. He desperately wanted a Heart switch for the setting trick but how could he convey that message. Normally, discarding a high card would be a signal for a switch to that suit but unfortunately East only had the three lowest cards in Hearts. So, East displayed one of the major attributes of a good defender. He took the need to guess out of partner's mind. He trumped partner's good ♦Queen and cashed the top Heart for the setting trick. It is worth noting that West was following good technique on his part. On the third trick, West led the high Diamond hoping to get a signal from partner as to what suit to lead next. If he had wanted to give East a ruff at that point, he would have led the 3.

The second hand has a defender once again trumping partner's winner but this time it's an Ace. This is considered such a dastardly crime that it can lead to violence.

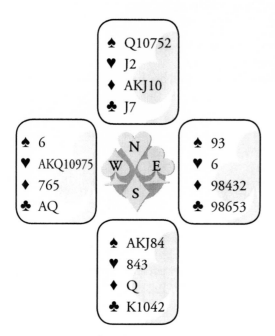

♠ Q10752
♥ J2
♦ AKJ10
♣ J7

♠ 6
♥ AKQ10975
♦ 765
♣ AQ

♠ 93
♥ 6
♦ 98432
♣ 98653

♠ AKJ84
♥ 843
♦ Q
♣ K1042

After a Spade opening by South, a Heart overcall by West and a game bid in Spades by north, West led the ♥King, followed by the Ace. With such a worthless hand R.H.O. was more anxious to get on to the next hand than he was to give this one any thought. However, being a dutiful partner, he brought all the brain cells he could muster to his worthless collection of pointed and rounded, red and black spots. Looking at the dummy, he reasoned that after two Heart tricks things looked pretty bleak for the defence. The only hope lay in Clubs. So, East trumped his partner's Ace on trick two and led a Club. He knew, so he went. End of story.

In this last hand, it is not a defender doing what is necessary, it is a Declarer. Executing the required play is not difficult but recognizing it as the best solution and then following your convictions is not what an unthinking Declarer would do.

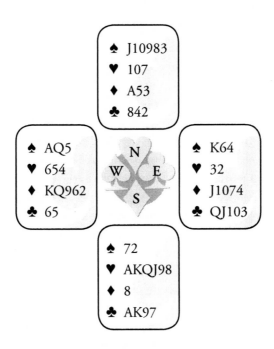

Contract: 4♥   Opening Lead: ♦K

Although there would appear to be only three losers – two ♠ and a ♣ – there could be a fourth if Clubs didn't break 3/3 and Declarer made the mistake of drawing trump too quickly. Declarer has to be very careful to win the opening lead and play three rounds of Clubs immediately. This will allow Declarer to trump the fourth round in dummy before drawing trump. Even if defender leads a trump when winning the third round of Clubs, it will be too little too late. But notice what a trump lead would accomplish if made on the opening lead. A second trump lead when winning the third Club would eliminate the Club ruff and defeat the contract. Aspiring Bridge players must stop living in the dark ages of Bridge and play trump on the opening lead far more often than is done.

Don't Suffer From That Common Ailment – Cold Feet

"Whose bid is it?"

14) LEADING PARTNER'S SUIT

There is very little in this game requiring more thought than the opening lead. Playing a hand, as Declarer, is much easier than as a defender. Since Declarer can see all his assets – dummy's hand is on the table – he has a marked advantage over defenders who can only see half of theirs. However, that opening lead gives the defence a jump start to the finish line and that advantage shouldn't be squandered by leading according to clichés of yesteryear. Although there are many – some good, some bad – nothing can replace thinking for yourself. And here are two of the bad ones. As beginners, players are taught to lead the fourth highest from their strongest and longest against a N.T. contract. What if their longest is not the strongest or visa versa or their hand is so worthless that cashing tricks, because of having no entries, would be impossible? A second one is the absolute lunacy of leading the highest in partner's suit, regardless of length in that suit. Here's one example of the many in existence of such dogmatic incompetence. The minute the

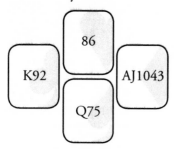

King hits the table on the opening lead, the Queen has become a trick for Declarer. Had the two been led and that would be automatic if this had been a side suit, the Queen would be history. And this is the essence of leading partner's suit from the get go. With just one exception, leading partner's suit is no different than leading any other. Since leading charts abound in Bridge books, instead of viewing another, let's just examine the general guidelines in choosing the opening lead and that one exception in partner's suit. Looking at the opening leader's options, let's first see some positive suggestions.

1. Lead the top of a sequence, whether solid or broken. A solid sequence is three cards in succession like this:

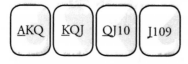

A broken sequence has the third card missing.

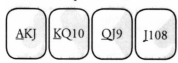

2. Lead the top of an interior sequence. An interior sequence is missing the second card. Some of these require partnership agreement because there are those who play coded 9's and 10's or Jack denies, ten implies.

3. Lead third or fourth highest from one or two non-touching honours. Notice the absence of an Ace.

4. Lead the top of touching honours.

5. Top of nothing. Make sure that on the second round of this suit that you play the middle card. If you play the bottom card second, partner might think it's a Doubleton.

6. Top of a worthless Doubleton. Notice the use of the word *'Worthless'*. Leading an honour which is the top card of a Doubleton is a losing strategy.

The above suggestions, although not a complete list can be used against N.T. or suit contracts. And quite often these guidelines can be utilized on the lead to subsequent tricks in the hand.

Now, to the exception when leading partner's suit. Although leading the top card from an honour Doubleton in a side suit is frowned upon it is the accepted wisdom in leading partner's suit.

And here are some negatives to observe when making the opening lead.

If We Are Content To Live In The Past, We Have No Future

1. Don't underlead an Ace against a suit contract.

2. Don't lead an unsupported Ace against a suit contract. Here's why – *'IYLAUAYSDWYSHL'*. Although this is considered an acronym, the origin of which I'm not aware, it's more like hieroglyphics. Deciphered it says, 'If you lead an unsupported Ace you'll soon discover what you should have led.' Remember this one!

The two reasons for not leading partner's suit:
1. You don't have any.
2. You don't like this partner.

15) TRUMP LEADS

This is without a doubt, the most difficult of yesteryear's habits to break. For the dark ages of Bridge, leading trump was considered the height of stupidity. Yet, today one of the world's most foremost writers and teachers has drawn up a list which shows 17 times when leading trump is a winning strategy and only four where it is inadvisable. These overwhelming odds continue to be ignored by too many players to their detriment. Without going into many specifics here are the guidelines which should be observed by more Bridge players.

The best way to defend a Bridge hand, especially on the opening lead is to put yourself in Declarer's seat. If the bidding has indicated a solid suit in dummy, one on which Declarer would be discarding losers, the defenders had better get their tricks while the getting's good. If a relatively weak dummy is likely to appear, the defence would be well advised to adopt a passive approach and not give tricks away. However, if Declarer is likely to be trumping losers in an effort to eliminate them, leading trump will save the day. And if one of your arguments against doing so is that you might be finessing partner, look for another excuse. Paraphrasing a leading teacher, writer and lecturer, "Find a reason to lead trump, instead of an excuse to avoid doing so." And, if a trump lead will finesse yourself it might still be a winning strategy.

Here are some of those specifics.

1. They've landed in a secondary suit.

2. One of your opponents has shown a preference in one of partner's suits.

3. You are strong in Declarer's suit(s).

4. Your side has opened N.T.

These are but a few of the reasons for leading trump. And of the four which make trump leads poor choices, dummy having a solid suit is the principle one.

We must remember, when declaring, that establishing a suit for discards and drawing trump are basic techniques. Therefore, if dummy already has a runnable suit, helping Declarer to draw trump is suicidal. Should you wish a much more complete treatment of the reasons for trump leads, one of my previous books, *'The 7 Deadly Sins of Bridge'* covers the topic extensively.

New Ideas Are
Often Blocked By
Old Ones

16) DOUBLETON HONOURS

When something unusual happens at the table, be that in the bidding or play, it should cause the others to quickly take notice. For example, bids such as Michael's, the unusual N.T. and splinters to name just three are quickly noticed. In play when a defender leads a low card like a 'two' from a known long suit, it has a message for partner. Similarly, when a defender leads a King followed by the Ace when, by agreement the partnership leads the Ace first, this also has a message for partner. Such a reversal shows a Doubleton. And, as will be seen in the following hand, the same message is sent by leading the Queen followed by the King.

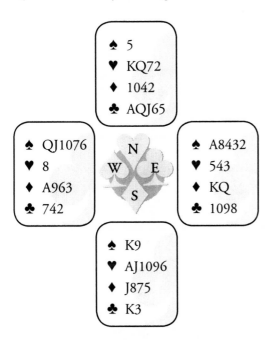

♠ 5
♥ KQ72
♦ 1042
♣ AQJ65

♠ QJ1076
♥ 8
♦ A963
♣ 742

♠ A8432
♥ 543
♦ KQ
♣ 1098

♠ K9
♥ AJ1096
♦ J875
♣ K3

Contract: 4♥

Opening Lead: ♠Q

After taking the Ace on trick one, East paused to take stock. The defence was unlikely to get any Spade, Heart or Club tricks. Even if partner had the ♣King it was finessable. It seemed to East that a Diamond switch, up to dummy's weakness was the only logical return, hoping partner had the Ace. The only other Ace West could have was the trump and that was most unlikely.

Yet that would only yield two more tricks which wouldn't be enough to defeat Declarer. So, East put on his thinking cap. If leading the King from A/K would indicate a Doubleton. Wouldn't leading the Queen from K/Q convey the same message. So our hero led the Queen. When the King appeared, the message wasn't lost on West. He overtook it, gave partner the ruff and when last seen our dynamic duo were high fiving as they waltzed out the door of the Club.

17) RUFFING PARTNER'S TRICK

We've all heard the old joke about the Bridge player who showed up at the Club with some sort of injury and was asked if he had trumped his partner's Ace. And just as other guidelines in this game can be ignored when certain situations dictate, so it is with the trumping of partner's trick. The following hand is a very dramatic example of someone doing just that and ending up wearing a crown instead of a bandage.

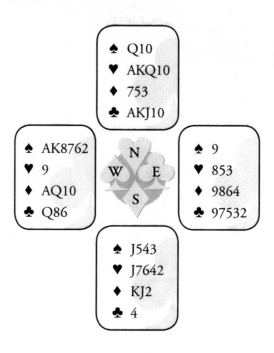

♠ Q10
♥ AKQ10
♦ 753
♣ AKJ10

♠ AK8762
♥ 9
♦ AQ10
♣ Q86

♠ 9
♥ 853
♦ 9864
♣ 97532

♠ J543
♥ J7642
♦ KJ2
♣ 4

Contract: 4♥   Opening Lead: ♠A

With this quite normal contract and equally normal opening lead, one would expect Declarer to have no trouble. However, east, our hero could never be accused of playing like a robot. He realized that those powerful Clubs in dummy would easily take care of any losing Diamonds which Declarer might have (even if partner had the ♣Queen it was finessable).

So, genius that he was, he trumped partner's King on trick two and led the ♦9. As a result, Declarer lost the first four tricks and had to congratulate East on a well-executed defence.

18) TRUMP PROMOTION

Whether declaring or defending, timing of plays is extremely critical in a high percentage of hands. For example, if Declarer is planning to cross-ruff a hand, it is of the utmost importance that he cash side suit winners before embarking on the cross-ruff. From the defenders' side, as most Bridge players know, giving a ruff and sluff is normally a lose/lose situation. However, allowing a ruff and sluff is not such a heinous crime if Declarer has no losers to sluff. He would only be sluffing a winner, a trick to which he was entitled in any event. Similarly, if a trump promotion seems like defenders' only road to success, it shouldn't be attempted until the defence has all the other tricks to which it is entitled. Trying for a trump promotion prematurely will simply allow Declarer to discard a loser. All the defence will have accomplished is the trading of winners with Declarer.

There are three basic ways to promote a trump trick for the defence – an uppercut, refusing a ruff and leading a suit which Declarer can ruff but third hand can overruff. The following hands will illustrate each of these types of trump promotions.

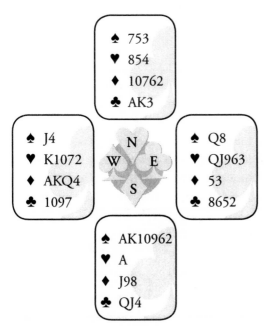

Contract: 4♠
Opening Lead: ♦A

West cashes the top Diamonds and begins looking for a fourth trick. With nothing better to do, he leads a fourth Diamond and east, bless his soul, trumps with the Queen, thereby promoting his partner's Jack to the setting trick because Declarer has to overruff. If you hold two worthless trump and can ruff a trick, do so with your highest.

You can never be sure of what might happen. You have nothing to lose. Your trump will soon be a footnote. In this hand, a defender has the opportunity to overruff but by refusing to do so, promotes a second trump trick for the defense.

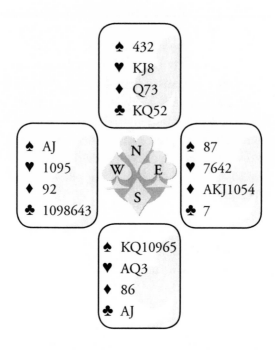

Contract: 4♠   Opening Lead: ♦9

After winning the first Diamond, with the 10, East continued with the Ace and King. Declarer had seen the Doubleton signal from West on the first two tricks and couldn't afford to trump low for fear of West winning with a low trump. The Ace of trump would then have become the setting trick. Declarer therefore trumped with the Queen, hoping to be overruffed by the Ace. But West had learned Bridge at his mother's knee and discarded instead. This meant that he was guaranteed two tricks for down one. Had West overruffed, as Declarer had hoped he would, West would have had to settle for the one trump and Declarer would have been the victor.

In this last hand, a slightly different trump promotion occurs. Refusing to overruff does not promote a second trump trick. In fact, it costs defender a trick.

Trumps Are The Soul Of The Game

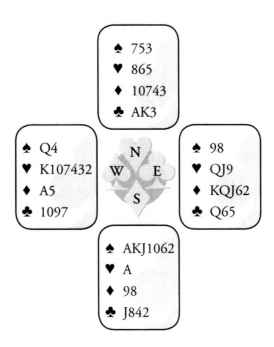

Contract: 4♠   Opening Lead: ♦A

When East won the second Diamond trick and led a third Diamond, Declarer's goose was cooked. If he trumped high, West's Queen was promoted. If he ruffed low, West would overruff. Either way the ♣Queen would be defender's fourth trick.

19) Setting Trick

Both newcomers and experienced players have their own peculiar inherent flaws. Newcomers, because they only think one trick at a time, take any tricks available very quickly and then begin looking for those extra ones needed. Experienced players are always looking for more from the beginning of play. And this is occasionally detrimental because there are times when you should take what is rightfully yours and be happy with your lot. Just such carelessness manifests itself in another way – not making partner's play easy for him. In *'Taking Control'* it was suggested that the defender who is aware of the direction which the defence should take should do so and not give partner an opportunity to make a bad guess. The following hand is a case in point.

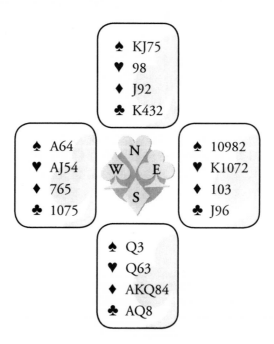

Contract: 3N.T.   Opening Lead: ♥4

After winning the King on the first trick, East returned the two (his original fourth highest). This told partner that East had started with four Hearts, meaning that Declarer had only three. Upon winning the Jack for a second Heart trick, West cashed the Ace and led to partner's known 10. This was the fourth trick for the defence and had East now led a Spade the contract would have been down one.

Unfortunately, East was reluctant to lead up to dummy's strength and chose a Diamond (up to dummy's weakness) and presumably through Declarer's strength. As a result, the contract was made. The culprit here was West as was pointed out in the post mortem. He could easily have relieved partner of a guess by cashing the ♠Ace before leading that fourth heart. He who knows, goes.

"I just can't believe I won first prize."

20) DECEPTION

Whether bidding, declaring or defending, being deceptive has its rewards. But it also has its penalties. When bidding or defending trying to deceive your opponent runs the risk of also deceiving your partner. Partner would forgive you instantly if your deception scored a top result. If it produced bad results, more often than not, forgiveness might never come. However, as a Declarer, you can't deceive partner. He's the dummy. Here are three basic Declarer deceptions.

1.

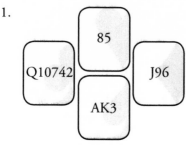

to L.H.O. in this N.T. contract.

When the 4 is led, R.H.O. contributes the Jack and you don't need to hold-up, win with the King. You're fooling no one if you play the Ace. But if you win with the King, your R.H.O. might think that you took it for fear of losing it

2.

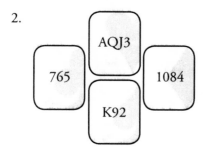

Wanting to cross to dummy, play the 9 to the Queen. To L.H.O. it might look like you were tempting him to cover with the 10. To R.H.O. it might look like his partner has the King. And since the 2 didn't appear on the first trick, both opponents will think partner has it and was showing an even number of cards.

3. The Bath Coup is as old as the game itself. We have all, in our Bridge infancy tried to perpetrate such a non-deceptive deception. Here it is again. L.H.O. leads the King from KQXX. As Declarer you hold AJX and contribute your spot in hopes that said L.H.O. will continue the suit giving you two tricks. Experienced players won't fall for this. However, they might if your holding was AJ72 and you played the 7 on the King, leading L.H.O. to think partner had the two and wanted a continuation. As always, be aware that holding-up in any circumstance might

convince the leader to switch with devastating results. While on the topic of the Bath Coup, I should point out that the modern game has a coup called the Bath Coup Buster which, as mentioned earlier, will be discussed later with other coups.

To close this part about Declarer's deceptive measures, a complete hand shows the wonder of such deception.

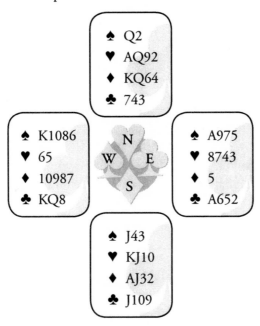

Contract: 3N.T.   Opening Lead: ♦10

Declarer has eight ironclad tricks in the red suits. Both black suits have glaring weaknesses. There are times when showing a little courage and attacking your own weak suit will throw the defenders off the scent. And this hand has just such an opportunity. A resourceful Declarer will win the first three tricks ending dummy and immediately lead a small Club toward the J109 in his own hand.

Cashing all the red suit winners allows defenders to make discards and discards allow signals. By trying the Clubs first, Declarer has a greater chance of a defender making a losing return upon winning that first Club. If the defence now leads and continues Spades, Declarer has his ninth trick. It would never occur to the defence that continuing Clubs would be logical.

After all, this is obviously a suit in which Declarer has some values which he is trying to maximize.

*Ah, Deception!
What A
Wonderful Toy!*

And here are some defensive deceptions which are more likely to deceive Declarer with minimal effect on partner.

1. From a holding such as J95, play the middle card in second seat. Declarer might play you for the Doubleton J/9.

2.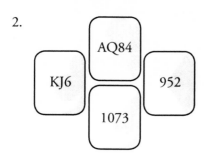

   Declarer leads the 3 and successfully finesses the Queen. When he plays the Ace next, drop your King. He knows you've got it and the King and Jack are equals so you're losing nothing while convincing Declarer that your partner has the Jack.

3.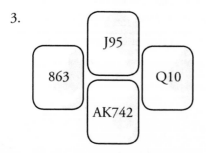

   This is the trump suit and Declarer leads the Ace. Drop your Queen under it. You'd be amazed how many Declarers will now finesse partner for the 10.

Following are additional deceptions which are worthy of note.

1. Just as a defender, in third seat, should play the lower of touching honours a Declarer should play the higher one from the closed hand. The reader's intelligence shouldn't be insulted by further explanation.

2. As Declarer, even though it makes no difference to you, lead an honour if you want it covered. A defender might place an honour which you are concealing in his partner's hand.

3. Even though you don't need signals to inform partner giving signals to defenders is often advantageous. Treat a defender as your partner. If you want a suit continued, signal encouragement.

4. Hiding a spot card might steer defender away from a ruff or confuse a count.

5. Although running a long suit early in N.T. play causes defenders to make discards before they have a better count of the hand, it does have a down side – signals. Perhaps you could lead another suit, thereby suggesting that it is the better one.

6. Make your opponents think you are tempting a cover even if you are not. This is a good ploy for a defender or Declarer.

21) PROJECTION

Just as Declarer must do whatever is necessary to bring in a seemingly hopeless contract, so must defenders do whatever is humanly possible to accomplish what appears to be a hopeless task.

As has already been observed in this section 'Born of Necessity' and will be in 'Coups', Declarer or defenders must reject any pessimistic thoughts about the outcome of a particular contract and envision the only line of play which will lead to success. Although there are many ways in which projecting the play, from the declaring or defending side, can manifest itself, there can be no doubt that the following are near or at the top of the list.

As a Declarer, ducking or holding-up, handling card combinations properly and overtaking are important tools. A defender can add whether or not to return partner's suit and counting partner's distribution and/or points to those Declarer tools. The basic philosophy of a defender should be one of bidding's guidelines: 'He Who Knows, Goes.' In other words, if a defender knows how best to defend he should embark on that course and take the decision out of partner's hands. After all, partner might have no idea as to the best defence.

Although this last point has been mentioned at other times, it is so important that repeating it is worthwhile.

One of the basic guidelines to a successful defence is to not 'throw in the towel.' For those who are not familiar with this phrase from the pugilistic sports, it simply means to give up. Always assume you can defeat Declarer. It may be that Declarer has too many weapons and your cause is hopeless. However, more often than not, success goes to the side which takes full advantage of its assets.

This reminds me of the proverb:

'The Harder I Work, The Luckier I Get!'

Following are complete hands to illustrate the kind of thinking which must prevail if the defence is to succeed.

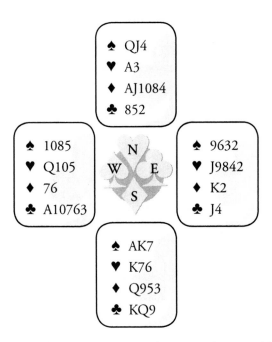

Counting winners reveals three ♠, two ♥ and one ♦. The extra three tricks needed can only come from Diamonds. However, simply winning the first trick and trying the Diamond finesse would be disastrous as back would come a Club – down one. But, if Declarer projects the play, he can simply let the Jack win trick one. When a Club is returned at trick two, L.H.O. will win but is completely stymied. Declarer now has an additional three Diamonds to go with his six original tricks.

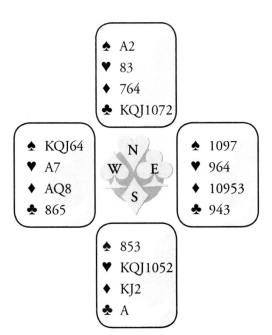

Contract: 4♥
Opening Lead: ♠K

It would appear that Declarer has four losers – one ♠, one ♥ and two ♦. The finessaholic would win trick one in dummy and immediately try the Diamond finesse. He would then blame the Bridge gods for going one off. Yet the contract was 100% guaranteed by simply projecting what a hold-up of the ♠Ace would accomplish. Declarer could win any continuation, unblock the ♣Ace and re-enter dummy with a Spade ruff and pitch two Diamonds on the established Clubs. But, does this line really guarantee success? What if L.H.O., after winning trick one, were to lead Ace and another Heart?

This hand is an example of how critical the handling of certain combinations can be.

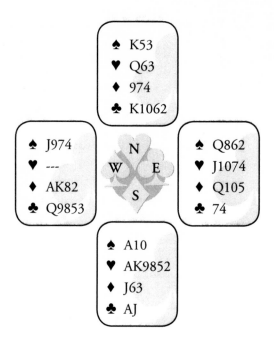

With defenders having taken the first three tricks in Diamonds, Declarer's only problem, although many wouldn't see it, was avoiding a trump loser. Admittedly, a 4 – 0 trump break would happen seldom but that is exactly what a good Declarer considers. As can be seen, if all four are on the left, Declarer's cause is hopeless.

However, if they are on the right, Declarer can cope. After winning trick four Declarer must lead to the trump Queen in dummy. Once L.H.O. shows out, Declarer can take the marked finesses against R.H.O. and all because he projected a scenario which could be resolved if necessary. Notice that Declarer maintained a tenace in the only hand which had one. And this is why nothing could have been done if L.H.O. had the four missing trump. There was no tenace in dummy.

The next two hands show first a Declarer and then a defender overtaking a trick which was already won on the other side of the table. This was because they had projected a line of play which necessitated a lead from the other hand.

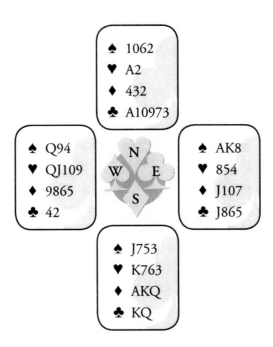

Contract: 3N.T.   Opening Lead: ♥Q

Counting winners, Declarer has two ♥, three ♦ and three ♣ – not enough.
However, even getting three Clubs let alone the additional one which is
needed is not an easy task. And all because those dastardly defenders have
attacked the suit which has the only side entry to dummy.   As a result,
Declarer has to overtake a winner to collect his nine tricks. Declarer has to
win the first trick in hand and immediately lead the ♣King and overtake
the Queen so that Clubs can be continued from dummy. Once the third
Club was lost to the Jack, the other two became winners with the carefully
preserved ♥Ace as the entry to them.

This hand, the defensive overtake, is a classic example of how the defender
who knows what line of play should be undertaken by the defence, assumes
control.

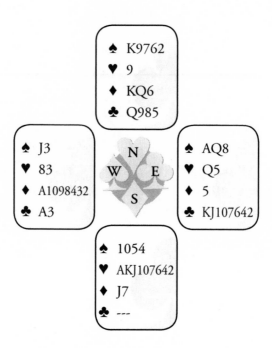

After an opening of 3 Diamonds, South bid 3 Hearts and became Declarer. The opening lead was the Jack of Spades. Because the opening lead was likely a Doubleton, East could envision two Spades and a Spade ruff for three tricks. If partner had the ♦Ace, it, plus a Diamond ruff would set the contract.

However, West could not possibly see the defence taking this line so that East took control. He played his Queen on the opening lead and returned his Singleton Diamond. It didn't take West long to clue in. He took the ♦Ace and gave his partner the ruff. East now cashed the ♠Ace and led a Spade for partner to ruff. A well thought out defence led to a one trick set of a contract that would easily make against lesser defenders.

The next hand requires a defender to break from the norm, something which is foreign to too many players.

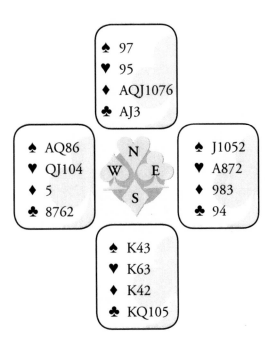

♠ 97
♥ 95
♦ AQJ1076
♣ AJ3

♠ AQ86
♥ QJ104
♦ 5
♣ 8762

N
W　E
S

♠ J1052
♥ A872
♦ 983
♣ 94

♠ K43
♥ K63
♦ K42
♣ KQ105

Contract: 3N.T.　Opening Lead: ♥Q

Too many players are very dogmatic in their approach to the game. To not return partner's suit would be unthinkable to these types. They never seem to realize when Declarer makes a contract that it might be because they didn't look elsewhere instead of returning partner's suit. In this hand, if East were to win the first trick and follow the age-old advice of returning partner's suit, Declarer would have no trouble rattling off 11 tricks. Since East has no Diamond or Club honours the minors should make him realize that even if partner has them they are finessable. That being the case, a Heart return to Declarer's marked King and at least seven tricks in the minors makes defeating 3N.T. a tall order. Following such analysis should make East realize that the only possibly profitable return is the ♠Jack. Once again, projecting and leading up to weakness wins the day.

This last hand requires that a defender make what might appear to be a suicidal switch. However, upon closer analysis proves to be, not only an absolute necessity but a stroke of genius as well.

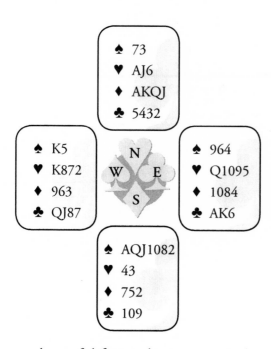

♠ 73
♥ AJ6
♦ AKQJ
♣ 5432

♠ K5
♥ K872
♦ 963
♣ QJ87

♠ 964
♥ Q1095
♦ 1084
♣ AK6

♠ AQJ1082
♥ 43
♦ 752
♣ 109

Contract: 4♠
Opening Lead: ♣7

As is very often the case, it is how each side utilizes its assets which determines the outcome of a hand. And here the defence has no time to lose. Upon winning the first two Club tricks, East must realize that those formidable Diamonds in dummy offer Declarer a parking place for a loser or two from his hand. Since there is no future in continuing Clubs, East must look to the Hearts for any hope of defeating the contract. And yet, as most Bridge players have been taught, leading up to a tenace is a good imitation of insanity. However, East must bite the bullet, lead the ♥10 and hope that partner can force the Ace leaving our hero with the Q/9 sitting over the Jack. The lead of the 10 promises the 9 and often a higher non-touching card. West can see that his partner must have the Queen. Otherwise why would he be making such a losing lead. Upon winning Declarer's losing trump finesse, West can return a Heart for a one trick set. Any other return at trick three would allow Declarer to bring in the game contract by discarding his Heart loser on dummy's fourth Diamond. Admittedly, East was playing his partner to have the ♥King as well as a winning trump. But that's what winning defence is all about – projecting the only distribution of the cards which could lead to success.

*Patience
And Tenacity
Far Outweigh
Cleverness*

22) OVERTAKING

Of the many definitions for this word, the only one which could possibly apply to Bridge is 'to do better in competition'. To overtake is simply to win a trick which has already been won by the opposite hand. And this is so whether declaring or defending. As a Declarer, you win a trick which would have belonged to dummy had you played low and visa versa. As a defender, partner has already played the highest to the trick when you play in fourth seat. However, you play a higher card, either deliberately or of necessity. Regardless of your position at the table, declaring or defending, partner's initial reaction is one of shock, "Why would partner play a higher card?" And the answer is usually that partner wants to lead to the next trick, either to avoid an end play, to continue a suit which the opposite hand couldn't do, to make a switch or to prevent partner making a mistake. All of these principles will be illustrated by hands but before doing so, let's look at a hand which combines the overtaking technique with a little chicanery.

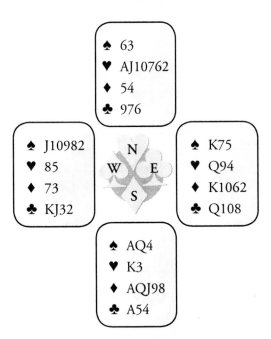

♠ 63
♥ AJ10762
♦ 54
♣ 976

♠ J10982
♥ 85
♦ 73
♣ KJ32

♠ K75
♥ Q94
♦ K1062
♣ Q108

♠ AQ4
♥ K3
♦ AQJ98
♣ A54

Contract: 3N.T.
Opening Lead: ♠J

As can be readily seen, Declarer needs dummy's Hearts to bring home this borderline contract. However, that never-ending problem of entries rears its ugly head once again. Solving this dilemma requires a little thought and ducking a trick to the defenders, to maintain an entry, combined with overtaking wins the day. Because of the opening lead, Declarer has two Spades and with a successful finesse of Diamonds, three more tricks. Adding two Hearts and a Club brings the total to eight – not enough. Obviously, an additional trick can only come from Hearts but cashing the King and finessing not only fails but eliminates one of the original eight tricks. Better to enlist the aid of an unsuspecting defender. At trick two, Declarer finesses for the ♥Queen, wins any return, overtakes his ♥King and runs home with ten tricks. Poor East couldn't possibly know that ducking the Heart finesse was the correct play. His partner would play the 8 to the first Heart to show count but would also play it from the K – 8.

In this next hand, a defender, wanting to relieve partner of a difficult decision and feeling that a switch was in order, overtook partner's opening lead.

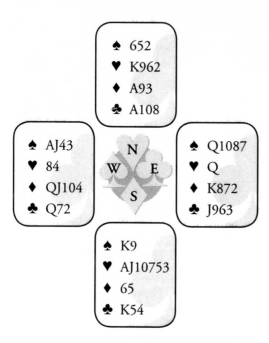

♠ 652
♥ K962
♦ A93
♣ A108

♠ AJ43
♥ 84
♦ QJ104
♣ Q72

♠ Q1087
♥ Q
♦ K872
♣ J963

♠ K9
♥ AJ10753
♦ 65
♣ K54

Contract: 4♥
Opening Lead: ♦Q

Declarer has a Club and Diamond loser and also two Spades if a Spade lead comes from R.H.O. Realizing that, said R.H.O. was the dangerous one, Declarer was planning an end play in Clubs against L.H.O. to force a Spade return. But a funny thing happened on the way to the finish line. R.H.O. was counting and realized that one Diamond (Declarer ducked the first trick) and a possible Club trick wouldn't be enough. If the defence was to prevail, two Spade tricks were an absolute. So, R.H.O. overtook partner's opening lead, led a Spade giving his side two more tricks. It was then just a matter of time before the defenders collected a Club trick for down one.

In the following hand, R.H.O. once again overtakes partner's opening lead. However, this time it's to make a switch for a different reason. Just as Declarer is well-advised to take losers early in an effort to establish a suit, so it is with defenders.

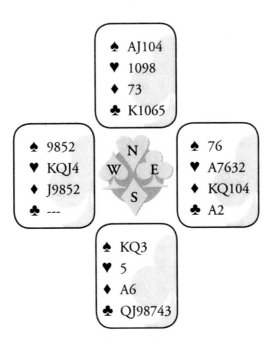

Contract: 5♣   Opening Lead: ♥K

East realized that, with a sure trump trick and the obvious Heart, another trick had to be found before Declarer could unload a loser or two on dummy's Spades. Having no Spade values himself meant that any values partner might have were finessable. Needing to act quickly, he overtook the ♥King and led the ♦King. Squirm as he might, Declarer couldn't avoid a loser in Hearts, one in Diamonds and the trump Ace.

In this hand, a defender needing a ruff to defeat the contract overtakes the opening and leads his Singleton. He has a guaranteed entry in trump and can get back to partner by leading to partner's ♥Queen. This is another example of how defenders are able to communicate because of trusting leads. The lead of the ♥King promised the Queen. As a result, Declarer is down in a contract that can be made easily without the razor-sharp defence which was produced by the opponents.

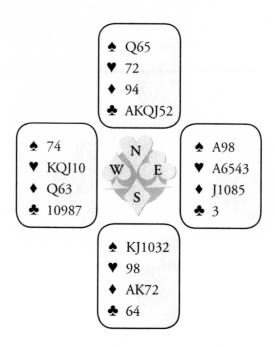

♠ Q65
♥ 72
♦ 94
♣ AKQJ52

♠ 74   N   ♠ A98
♥ KQJ10   W   E   ♥ A6543
♦ Q63   S   ♦ J1085
♣ 10987   ♣ 3

♠ KJ1032
♥ 98
♦ AK72
♣ 64

Contract: 4♠   Opening Lead: ♥K

As can be seen, if R.H.O. either encourages a continuation or plays low requesting a switch, hopefully to Clubs, there is no guarantee that the opening leader will understand or even comply. It's so much simpler for partner to overtake the opening lead and switch to his Singleton Club. When Declarer begins extracting trump, he can then take the Ace, lead to partner's known ♥Queen and receive his just reward – a Club ruff. This is such an easy game.

This final hand, illustrating a defensive overtake, is a N.T. contract.

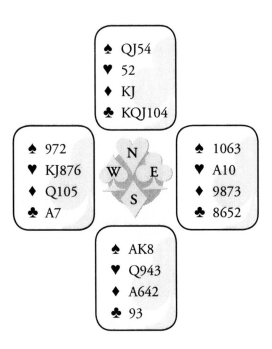

♠ QJ54
♥ 52
♦ KJ
♣ KQJ104

N
W E
S

♠ 972
♥ KJ876
♦ Q105
♣ A7

♠ 1063
♥ A10
♦ 9873
♣ 8652

♠ AK8
♥ Q943
♦ A642
♣ 93

Contract: 3 N.T.   Opening Lead: ♥7

Declarer has four ♠ tricks and two in ♦. Once the ♣Ace is dislodged, there are four more Club trucks making ten tricks in all. Seeing those excellent Clubs in dummy should be all the warning the defenders need. 'Time's-A-Wastin'! The defence should get their ducks in a row quickly. So, when his partner wins the first trick and returns the ten, the opening leader should overtake with the Jack and continue with the King. This establishes Declarer's Queen as a trick but also establishes West's last Heart as the setting trick when he gets in with the ♣Ace (four ♥ and the ♣). Declarer employed proper technique by refusing to play the Queen on the second trick. He was giving the defender to his left a chance to go wrong by not overtaking but unfortunately L.H.O. was up to the task. A second point to note here is that R.H.O. after winning the first trick would still lead the 10 from an original holding of A-10-X. If that were the case, L.H.O. should still overtake with the Jack and cash the King. In that scenario, Declarer's Queen would fall and then the contract would be down two.

23) SMOTHER PLAY

There are a number of ways in which Declarer can overcome what appears to be a certain trump trick for the defence. One is the *'Devil's Coup'* and another is the *'Trump Coup'* (both of which will be discussed in greater detail later). A third is the above title. However, there are certain card combinations in every suit, including trump, which enable a Declarer or defender to smother another's card and gain in the process. This other use of the word 'Smother' will be the focus of this section.

1.

xxxx
KJ109

With no entries to the top hand, making a finesse impossible, lead the King. This might be your lucky day, a stiff Queen.

2.

xxxx
Q1098

Same as above. You might find the Jack alone.

3.

A
Q1098xx

Play the Ace and enter the bottom hand in another suit. Lead the Queen. The Jack might now be alone.

4.

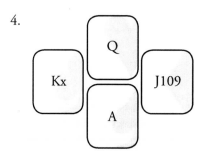

Q
Kx
J109
A

Part way through a hand and knowing that partner has some values in this suit, lead the King.

5.

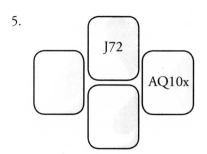

J72
AQ10x

A dummy surround play. Lead the Queen.

Many players like to cover an honour with an honour. By doing so, they are getting two of the opponents honours for one of theirs. Whether or not this is a winning play depends on the particular circumstances at the time and is not being debated here (next section). However, wouldn't you agree that you are accomplishing precisely the same in this type of smother play?

COUPS

A Successful Stroke Or Stratagem

1) LEAD-DIRECTING DOUBLE

Newer players who are trying to get a grasp of this game are aghast when informed that there are more than ten types of doubles. And although this one might not be considered as a coup, in the strictest sense, its value as a strategic bid is tremendous.

As mentioned, any bid, Declarer technique or defensive ploy can be adapted or broadened to a partnership's style. As a result, the following examinations are basic to most.

Doubling 3N.T.

When a 3N.T. contract is doubled by the defender, not on lead, it requests a lead of dummy's first suit. If dummy hasn't bid a suit (1N.T. – 3N.T.), the double requests a lead of leader's short major.

Doubling Artificial Bids

In each of the following examples, the double asks partner to lead the doubled suit.

- Double of a Stayman Inquiry – lead a ♣

- Double of a 2 ♣ opening – lead a ♣

- Double of a Transfer (2 ♦ or 2 ♥) – lead this suit

- Double of a Blackwood response – lead this suit

- Double of a Splinter Bid – lead the higher ranking side suit

Don't let what you cannot do interfere with what you can.

Doubling A Freely-Bid Slam

This double specifically asks for an unusual lead.

- Not trump or an unbid suit

- Dummy's first suit

- Doubler has a void, find it

"I double!"

2) COUP EN PASSANT

This is a term taken from chess. As it applies to Bridge it means winning a trick with a trump which is not the highest one still in the game. This definition is similar to Oswald Jacoby's definition of a successful finesse. To accomplish this feat, Declarer must lead a side suit through the hand of a defender who has the higher trump. The following examples are all two or three card end positions.

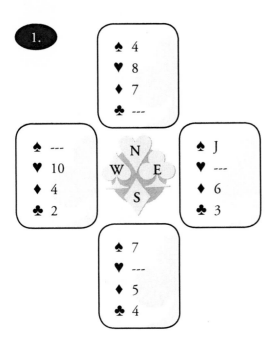

In this example Spades are trump and dummy's on lead. By leading a suit in which he is void, Declarer is able to win with his ♠7 and so he leads the ♥8.

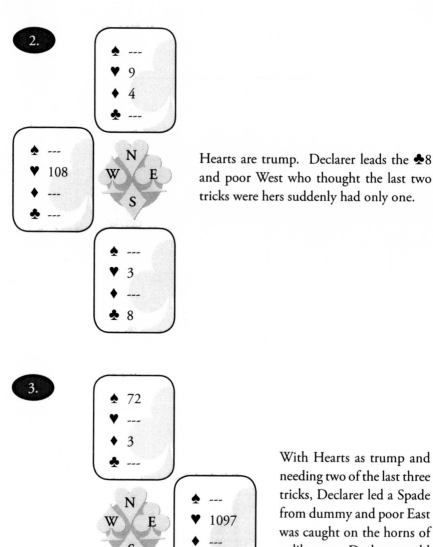

2.

♠ ---
♥ 9
♦ 4
♣ ---

♠ ---
♥ 108
♦ ---
♣ ---

♠ ---
♥ 3
♦ ---
♣ 8

Hearts are trump. Declarer leads the ♣8 and poor West who thought the last two tricks were hers suddenly had only one.

3.

♠ 72
♥ ---
♦ 3
♣ ---

♠ ---
♥ 1097
♦ ---
♣ ---

♠ ---
♥ Q8
♦ J
♣ ---

With Hearts as trump and needing two of the last three tricks, Declarer led a Spade from dummy and poor East was caught on the horns of a dilemma. Declarer could not be prevented from winning two trump tricks.

4.

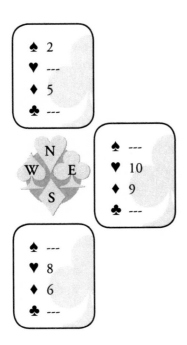

♠ 2
♥ ---
♦ 5
♣ ---

♠ ---
♥ 10
♦ 9
♣ ---

♠ ---
♥ 8
♦ 6
♣ ---

With Hearts as trump, Declarer was in dummy to lead to this 12th trick. The Spade was led and Declarer collected his game-going trick with the ♥8, another *'Coup En Passant'*.

"We made it!"

3) SCISSORS

As the name implies you are cutting. But in this case it's communication not hair. Although there are other reasons for cutting the defender's lines of communication the most common is to prevent an impending ruff. And the most common manifestation of this coup is the loser-on-loser play. Here's a hand to illustrate this coup by utilizing a loser-on-loser play.

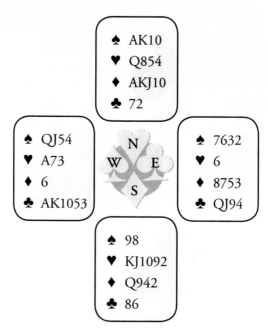

Contract: 4♥   Opening Lead: ♣Ace

Not only is this hand illustrating a 'scissor's coup' it is also demonstrating a conventional signal. On the opening lead, East played the Queen. This tells partner that the Queen is Singleton or the hand also contains the Jack. Either way East can win the second round. Knowing this, West led his Singleton Diamond to trick number two. West's defensive plan was to win the first trump lead, put East on lead with a Club and get a Diamond ruff for the setting trick. But Declarer had been watching the proceeding very carefully and took countermeasures. Upon winning trick two, Declarer played the Ace and King of Spades, followed by the 10 on which he discarded his remaining Club. This made it impossible for West to reach his partner's hand, via a Club, for the killing Diamond ruff. Declarer had executed a 'scissor's coup', cutting communications, by playing a loser (♣8) on a loser (♠10).

4) MORTON'S FORK

As you continue through this section on Coups, the exotic names begin to reverberate in your mind. However, this one, also known as the *'Dilemma Coup'* is probably the most riveting. It is named after Cardinal John Morton, Tax Collector for Henry VII. He had a unique outlook. Morton felt that the rich could afford to pay and that the poor were really the rich who were concealing their bounty. Both groups had to pay and were said to be impaled on Morton's fork. And that is precisely why a defender finds himself East of a rock and West of a hard place when Declarer makes that critical play – on the horns of a dilemma or impaled, if you will. In the following example hand, a couple of instructive play guidelines present themselves – don't be too quick to take a discard and lead through the defender whom you suspect has the Ace in a critical suit.

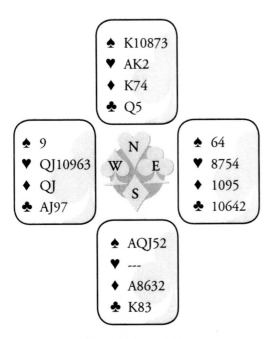

Contract: 6♠

Opening Lead: ♥Q

With L.H.O. having overcalled two Hearts when Declarer opened one Spade, it didn't require too much grey matter to place the ♣Ace in that hand. Therefore, eventually leading towards the ♣Queen was an odds on favourite to succeed. This is one of the instructive guidelines which was mentioned earlier. The other is that winning the opening lead in dummy and discarding from the other hand is seldom the correct play. Later in the hand a better discard is usually more obvious. Counting losers, Declarer can see an immediate one in Clubs and an eventual one in Diamonds. Seldom can you do anything about the immediate type so Declarer's efforts must be directed at eliminating the eventual one. Having processed all these thoughts, Declarer should trump the opening lead, draw trump with the Ace and Queen and lead a Club towards the Queen. West is rendered helpless.

If he takes the Ace, dummy's losing Diamond is eventually discarded on the ♣King. If he ducks, dummy's Queen wins and the two high Hearts become the parking places for Declarer's remaining Clubs.

5) Merrimac

This coup, although similar to the Deschapelles which follows in #6, is different in its purpose. The Merrimac deliberately sacrifices a sure trick in an effort to scuttle Declarer's plan of running a long suit in dummy by removing an entry to it.

You'll Always Miss Success If You Miss The Opportunity

Contract: 3N.T.
Opening Lead: ♦Ace

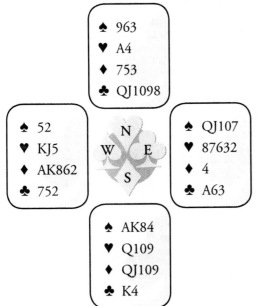

North
♠ 963
♥ A4
♦ 753
♣ QJ1098

West
♠ 52
♥ KJ5
♦ AK862
♣ 752

East
♠ QJ107
♥ 87632
♦ 4
♣ A63

South
♠ AK84
♥ Q109
♦ QJ109
♣ K4

Left to his own devices, Declarer would likely score four ♣, two ♦, one ♥ and two ♠ for nine tricks. However, upon taking the opening lead, West quickly realized that dummy's Clubs were potentially many tricks for Declarer and had to be neutralized. West also realized that the ♥Ace was probably the only entry to those Clubs.

As a result West sacrificed his ♥King and by giving partner a count signal when Declarer led Clubs, Declarer only managed one Club trick from that long suit. Of course, if Declarer refused to take the ♥King, West would simply lead another one. And if Declarer was still able to bring in the Club suit, the defence would have given up an overtrick with the Heart lead. But the effort to scuttle the Club suit would still have been worth the risk. Incidentally, this coup is appropriately named. The Merrimac was a ship deliberately sunk to block a harbour during the Spanish-American War.

6) DESCHAPELLES

As mentioned in *'Merrimac'* this coup is similar yet different. Here a defender deliberately sacrifices a sure trick in an effort to create an entry to partner's hand.

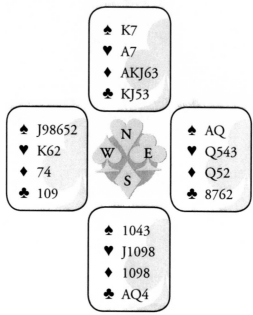

Contract: 3N.T.   Opening Lead: ♠6

After taking the first two tricks, East wondered how he might get back to partner and all those Spade tricks. Examining each suit, in turn, made him realize that Diamonds were hopeless. And if partner had the ♣Ace (highly unlikely) it wouldn't go away. This led East to the conclusion that West's entry could only be in Hearts. So East led his ♥Queen. When Declarer tried the Diamond finesse which was a necessity, East took his Queen and led a Heart to partner's King and the contract was down two. A Club return, by east, at trick three would have handed Declarer his contract.

Success Favours The Prepared Mind

7) VIENNA

While we have defenders in a magnanimous frame of mind and giving away certain tricks, let's turn our attention to just such a charitable gesture by Declarer – deliberately setting up a trick for a defender. In an earlier section on the use of a squeeze play, mention was made of how a defender has both busy and idle cards. At the point where a defender has no more idle cards to contribute to a trick, he must part with a busy card. The letting go of a busy card creates another winner for Declarer. As the reader will recall, one of the prerequisites to a successful squeeze is to be within one trick of your goal. So as soon as said defender parts with that busy card all is well for Declarer.

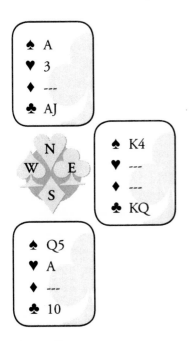

Here is a typical end position. Declarer leads a small Spade to the Ace and R.H.O. can part with his 4. Now he has nothing but busy cards and when the Heart is led from dummy, he has to part with his winning Spade or leave a Club unprotected – a Hobson's Choice.

Don't Confuse This With The Mating Of Austrian Doves

If ever there was one, a basic definition of a *'Vienna Coup'* is that Declarer deliberately sets up a King for a defender and then squeezes him out of it.

8) CROCODILE

Here we're going to show a defender, once again in a giving mood. One of Declarer's techniques in bringing in a contract is an end play. In it, Declarer shapes the play in such a way as to throw a defender on lead when he must make a favourable return for Declarer. Just as in a squeeze, a defender has busy and idle cards, so it is with end plays. At the critical moment, the hapless defender has nothing but busy cards left and must lead one of them. In the following end position, partner comes to the rescue. However, it must be pointed out that executing this coup is much easier if you are the fourth to play to a trick. It is much easier said than done when you are in second seat. The contract is 4 Spades and Declarer has already lost one trick.

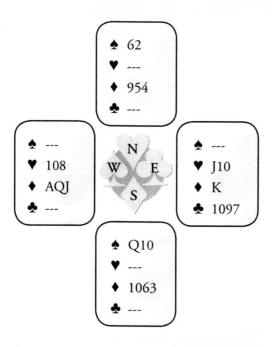

If East is forced to win a Diamond trick, he will have to lead a Heart or a Club, either of which gives Declarer a ruff and sluff as well as the contract. Therefore, if Declarer leads a Diamond from the dummy, West who has been watching play very carefully can overtake partner's King and cash two more Diamonds for down one. But if Declarer were to lead a Diamond from his own hand, it is much more difficult for West to know that he should take the Ace.

In Every Failure Is The Seed Of Success

9) Memory

Have you ever reached trick #12, as defender, with two winners in your hand and having to discard one of them? If you're not sure of which to keep, you are not alone. Most players have this happen to them quite frequently. The culprit – counting or lack thereof. You have just fallen victim to the *Memory Coup*.

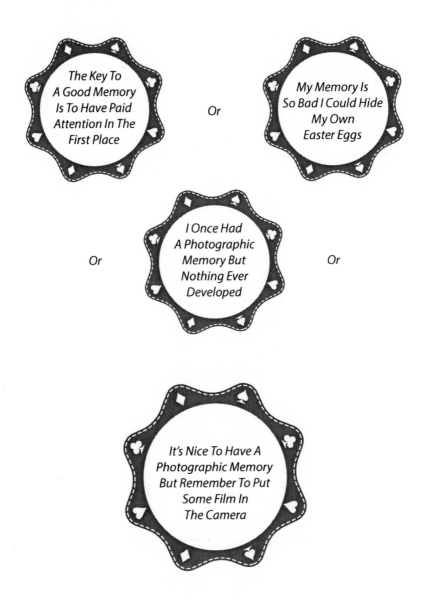

The Key To
A Good Memory
Is To Have Paid
Attention In The
First Place

Or

My Memory Is
So Bad I Could Hide
My Own
Easter Eggs

Or

I Once Had
A Photographic
Memory But
Nothing Ever
Developed

Or

It's Nice To Have A
Photographic Memory
But Remember To Put
Some Film In
The Camera

10) BATH COUP BUSTER

The *'Bath Coup'*, supposedly first perpetrated on an unsuspecting opponent in Bath, England, is the first coup learned by Bridge players. And when they exercised this technique they were likely unaware of having done anything special or that it had a name of its own. To refresh memories, here it is. When L.H.O. leads the King, a fairly common attacking lead, Declarer plays a small card from AJx, hoping that said L.H.O. will continue the suit and give him two tricks.

Today's players have come up with a countermeasure. They will lead the Queen from a holding such as the: KQ109(x). When partner sees the Jack in his own hand or dummy, the situation is immediately recognizable to him. If he has the Jack, he must drop it under partner's Queen. If he doesn't have it, he gives his count in that suit. If he has an odd number (3 or 5) he plays his smallest card, and if he has an even number (2 or 4) he plays a high card. And if the Jack is in the dummy, the opening leader will know, from partner's count signal, how best to continue. If it's in Declarer's hand, the leader will still have been provided with necessary information.

They Conquer Who Believe They Can

11) TRUMP

All Declarers know how to finesse. The more experienced know how not to finesse. Yet finesses are often necessary and must be executed properly. But a problem arises when you don't have a card to lead in the suit where a finesse is needed. For example, you have the ♦4 in one hand and the A/Q on the other side. It's a simple matter to lead the 4 and finesse. However if you don't have the 4 opposite the A/Q, finessing becomes another matter. And that is the essence of a trump coup. You successfully finesse against an opponent's supposed sure trump trick without a trump to lead. Here's a hand to illustrate this wonder.

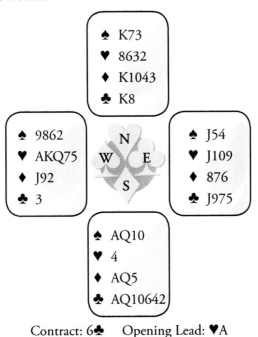

Contract: 6♣   Opening Lead: ♥A

Declarer trumps the second Heart and draws two rounds of trump, getting the bad news. It then became obvious to Declarer that only a trump coup would avoid the loss of a trump trick. However, there were a number of conditions necessary for this line of play to be successful. Declarer had to shorten his trump holding to the same number as the opponent who had the remaining outstanding trump. Defenders had to be good chaps and follow along as Declarer played out his side suit winners. Declarer had to be leading from dummy to trick #12. And, of course, Declarer had to have a tenace position over those outstanding trump. If they were in the opposite hand, Declarer's cause was hopeless.

After four tricks have been played, Declarer crosses to dummy and ruffs another Heart. Now, he cashes the remaining Diamonds and Spades, ending in dummy and the following end position has been reached.

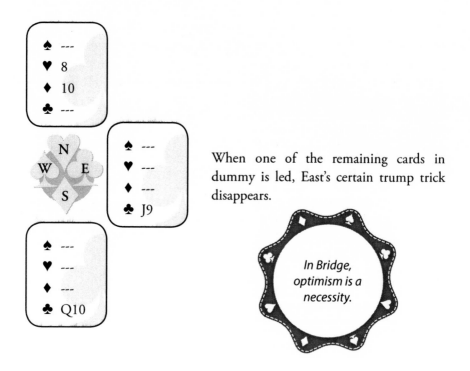

When one of the remaining cards in dummy is led, East's certain trump trick disappears.

In Bridge, optimism is a necessity.

12) LOSER-ON-LOSER

Although the lead-directing double and this play are not exotic sounding they do fit Webster's definition of a coup, which was highlighted on the title page. There are three principle reasons for employing this technique.

1. To maintain trump control

2. As preparation for a throw-in

3. To prevent a ruff or overruff

Following are hands to illustrate these three techniques.

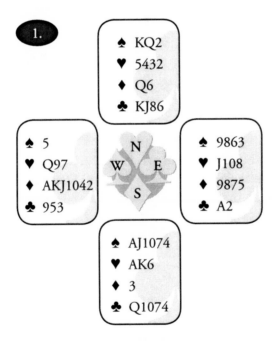

Contract: 4♠   Opening Lead: ♦Ace

Finessaholics see finesse, take finesse. The same applies to Declarers who see a ruff and take it, never considering the consequences which could very well be the loss of trump control with defeat following shortly after. In this hand, West starts with the Ace and King. The aforementioned ruffing Declarer would trump in his hand, and eventually fail because he would have no trump left for a Diamond continuation when he knocked out the ♣Ace. Better to trade losers by discarding a Heart on the second Diamond, a loser-on-loser play.

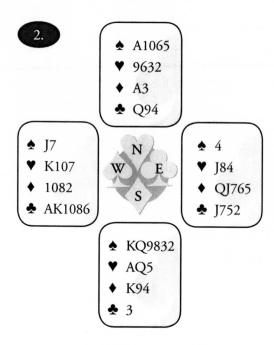

Contract: 6♠   Opening Lead: ♣Ace

Counting losers reveals two ♥ and one ♣. Rather than rely on a Heart finesse to eliminate a loser, Declarer embarked on an *'Elimination and Throw-In'*. Declarer trumped the Club continuation, drew trump, cashed the high Diamonds and trumped the last Diamond. At this point, he led the ♣Queen but instead of ruffing it, discarded the ♥five. West won but had to return a Heart into the Ace/Queen or yield a ruff and sluff.

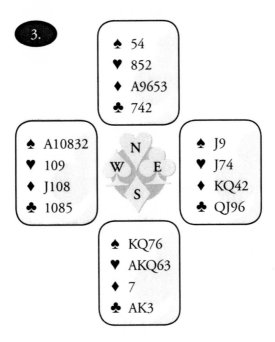

3.

North
♠ 54
♥ 852
♦ A9653
♣ 742

West
♠ A10832
♥ 109
♦ J108
♣ 1085

East
♠ J9
♥ J74
♦ KQ42
♣ QJ96

South
♠ KQ76
♥ AKQ63
♦ 7
♣ AK3

Contract: 4♥   Opening Lead: ♠Ace

Having seen East's Jack on the first round, West played a low Spade which Declarer won. But East's signal wasn't lost on Declarer. Knowing that he had to ruff a Spade in dummy and being afraid of an overruff, Declarer hit upon another line of play – a loser-on-loser. He led a Spade loser but instead of trumping it he discarded a Club from dummy. This enabled Declarer to ruff a Club in dummy instead of trying to trump a Spade, a play which was doomed.

There was another option which some Declarers might have tried. Declarer in this could have taken two rounds of trump before trying the Spade ruff. That would be done in the hope of exhausting East of trump. However, as can be seen East was the one holding a third trump. Another pertinent factor is worth mentioning. And that is the folly of leading an unsupported Ace on the opening lead – a mistake made by far too many Bridge players. The lead of a Heart or Diamond would have resulted in Declarer's demise.

13) Devil's

Can you imagine missing five trump including the Queen and Jack and not losing a trump trick. And no, those two honours are not Doubleton. They are actually distributed Jxx opposite Qx or Jx opposite Qxx. Enter the *Devil's Coup*, a magical trick that would make Houdini proud. However, be aware that performing this feat requires some preparation. And these prerequisites are similar to those required in executing other seemingly magical Bridge tricks.

For example and these are but a sampling:

1. If planning to cross-ruff a hand it is advisable to cash your side suit winners first.

2. To execute a trump coup, you must shorten your trump holding to that of your opponent.

3. If trying for a trump promotion, it is necessary to have taken all the winners to which you were entitled before attempting the promotion.

4. When planning a squeeze you must be just one trick shy of your goal and at the critical moment the opponents cannot have any idle cards left.

And so it is with the *Devil's Coup*. Declarer must not have more than three trump, normally two, when playing that critical card. Also, Declarer must have cashed all side suit winners by that critical moment.

You Can't Win By Conceding Defeat

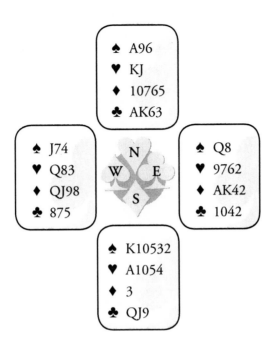

```
              ♠ A96
              ♥ KJ
              ♦ 10765
              ♣ AK63

♠ J74                        ♠ Q8
♥ Q83         N              ♥ 9762
♦ QJ98      W   E            ♦ AK42
♣ 875         S              ♣ 1042

              ♠ K10532
              ♥ A1054
              ♦ 3
              ♣ QJ9
```

Contract: 6♠   Opening Lead: ♦Q

After the Diamond lead was won, the suit was continued. Declarer trumped the second trick and surveyed the landscape. He was very tempted to quote Oliver Hardy, "This is another fine mess you've gotten me into Stanley." However, he soldiered on. The only hope was to avoid a trump loser, a tall order with 5 to the Q/J missing. But our hero had heard of this wonder play – he didn't know its name – which would eliminate that seemingly inevitable trump loser. He also remembered that he had to shorten his trump holding and cash side suit winners without ever leading trump. So he cashed the Ace and King of Hearts, ruffed a Heart, ruffed a Diamond, played three rounds of Clubs and ruffed one more Diamond. The following end position remained. Dummy had a Club and the A/9 of trump. L.H.O. had three Spades and R.H.O. two Spades and a Heart. South was on lead and led his last Heart. At this point, if they were playing chess, the King could be placed in a horizontal position. If L.H.O. trumped with the 7 or 4, dummy would overruff and claim the last two tricks with the A/K of trump. If L.H.O. trumped with the Jack, again dummy would overtrump and finesse against the Queen. Houdini had risen.

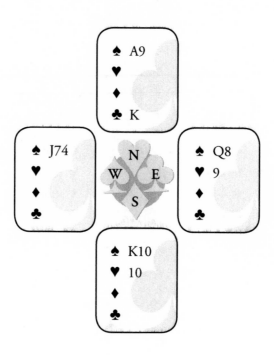

The Greater
The Obstacle,
The Greater
The Glory In
Overcoming It

DO IT
OR
ELSE

Keep Your Voids Separated From Other Suits

Much of what appears in this section was used partially or completely in previous sections. However, the importance of this material demands review.

1) PLANNING

For lack of study, they lacked knowledge.
For lack of knowledge, they lacked confidence.
For lack of confidence, they lacked success.

Preparing optimistically, whether declaring or defending, is absolutely paramount in the planning process. The inherent advantage that each side possesses might only be marginal and the eventual outcome of a hand most often depends on how the assets of each side are utilized rather than their relative strengths.

No Wind Serves Those Who Have No Destined Port

A good Declarer, in a suit contract, will begin by counting losers. If all seems in order, this Declarer will ask, "What can go wrong?" If a danger to the contract reveals itself countermeasures are taken. If the counting reveals that there aren't enough tricks for which the declaring side has contracted, Declarer should consider the following list of questions. They are not in a strict order of priority but those which appear at or near the beginning are the ones which will reveal the most common road to success.

A pessimist sees difficulty in every opportunity.
An optimist sees opportunity in every difficulty.

It Is More Important To Know Where You Are Going Than Where You Have Been

The Declarer's Side

1. **Can I trump losers in dummy?**

Dummy	Declarer
♠ QJ4	♠ AK1098
♥ Q965	♥ 3
♦ K743	♦ A85
♣ A2	♣ J753

Contract: 4♠
Opening Lead: ♦Q

Declarer must resist drawing the defenders' trump. He needs those in dummy to trump two Club losers.

2. **Are there any extra winners on which I could discard losers?**

Dummy	Declarer
♠ KQ53	♠ J
♥ QJ5	♥ K1097432
♦ A3	♦ 865
♣ A762	♣ Q4

Contract: 4♥
Opening Lead: ♦Q

Upon winning the first trick, Declarer must immediately use the ♠Jack to establish an extra Spade winner in dummy on which to discard a Club loser.

3. **Can I establish a suit in dummy on which to discard losers?**

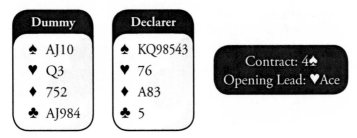

Dummy	Declarer	
♠ AJ10	♠ KQ98543	Contract: 4♠
♥ Q3	♥ 76	Opening Lead: ♥Ace
♦ 752	♦ A83	
♣ AJ984	♣ 5	

Declarer must trump the third Heart high in his hand, lead a Club to dummy and ruff a Club high again in his hand. He continues to enter dummy with a trump and ruffing Clubs high. After four rounds of Clubs, the fifth Club in dummy becomes established and allows for the discard of a Diamond loser. But Declarer must be careful to trump high in his hand. Not only can he not afford an overruff but he needs his low trump as entries to dummy.

4. **Maybe a loser-on-loser will work?**

Dummy	Declarer	
♠ KQJ3	♠ 6	Contract: 4♥
♥ 432	♥ AKQJ109	Opening Lead: ♣3
♦ 986	♦ AQ9	
♣ K75	♣ A6	

Take the opening lead in hand, draw trump and lead a Spade to the King. When it holds, lead the Queen and discard a Diamond. They can take the Ace but your other Diamond goes on the ♠Jack.

5. Do I need a hold-up?

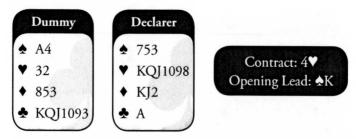

Dummy	Declarer
♠ A4	♠ 753
♥ 32	♥ KQJ1098
♦ 853	♦ KJ2
♣ KQJ1093	♣ A

Contract: 4♥
Opening Lead: ♠K

If Declarer wins the opening lead he goes down. By holding-up, the contract can't be defeated. See if you can explain it.

6. Maybe I could combine my chances?

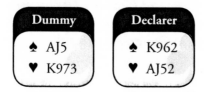

Dummy	Declarer
♠ AJ5	♠ K962
♥ K973	♥ AJ52

A successful finesse in either of these two isolated suits from your hand is needed to make your contract. But which one? With eight cards in one suit but only seven in the other, try dropping the missing Queen in the longer suit. If this fails, you can finesse in the other.

7. Who is the dangerous opponent?

Dummy	Declarer
♦ 4	♦ K5
♣ A1063	♣ KJ4

If one of the defenders was able to lead through your ♦King it would be an unwelcome situation. The one who could do that is the dangerous opponent. Keep him off lead by finessing through him in Clubs. If the Club finesse were to lose, the other defender couldn't attack Diamonds without making your King into a trick.

8. Do I need a finesse desperately enough to try one?

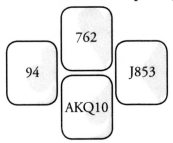

It is a wise Declarer, indeed, who finesses only as a last resort. However, if it is an absolute necessity, our wise Declarer will even try the following, one that most players wouldn't even consider. When missing six cards, they will likely split 4/2.

So, if you need all four tricks in this suit, finesse the 10. Most would try to drop the Jack. However, one defender will have two chances to be dealt the Jack while the other will have four, thus tipping the scales in favour of a finesse.

Chance favours the prepared mind.

9. Would an end play work?

Although this topic was covered in another section, its importance in the planning process cannot be overstated and further examination is certainly beneficial.

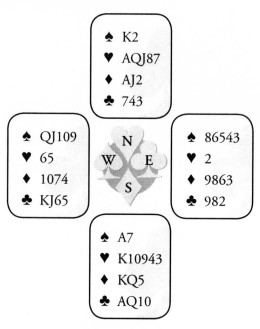

♠ K2
♥ AQJ87
♦ AJ2
♣ 743

♠ QJ109   N   ♠ 86543
♥ 65   W   E   ♥ 2
♦ 1074   S   ♦ 9863
♣ KJ65   ♣ 982

♠ A7
♥ K10943
♦ KQ5
♣ AQ10

Contract: 6♥   Opening Lead: ♠Q

Basically an end play requires that you strip or eliminate two suits from play, throw a defender in with a third suit and await your reward. In this hand, Declarer wins the opening lead and draws defenders' trump (strip #1). He then cashes the second Spade and all three Diamonds, ending in dummy. Then he finesses a Club and it doesn't matter if it's the Queen or 10. L.H.O. is now on lead and can choose his own route to oblivion. He can lead a Club up to Declarer's tenace or lead a pointed suit allowing Declarer to trump in dummy while discarding a Club loser from his hand. Notice that Declarer had to have trump left in dummy to still have the ruff and sluff option. In this case, you will have observed that Declarer actually stripped three suits – two from his own and dummy's hands and a third (trump) from defenders. Stripping three suits is not always necessary. Many times two is enough. In actual fact, the stripping process removes all defenders' idle cards so that whichever one of them is on lead has no way of throwing the lead back to Declarer. Idle cards are useless cards. Busy ones are either of value in their own right or as protectors of other cards.

10. Do I need a squeeze?

Just as end plays were covered previously and then examined again in this section on planning, so it is with the simple squeeze. It is certainly a very useful Declarer tool and bears repeating. But the end position should suffice.

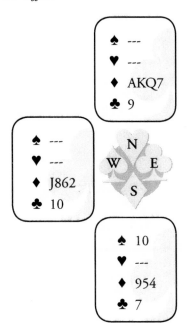

In this N.T. contract, needing all five remaining tricks, Declarer leads the ♣10 and L.H.O. is squeezed. If he parts with a Diamond, dummy discards a Club and the Diamonds take the rest of the tricks. If he discards a Club, dummy discards a Diamond with the same result.

11. **If I can't trump losers in dummy, perhaps I can trump them in hand (dummy reversal)?**

Dummy	Declarer
♠ QJ10	♠ AK952
♥ 1062	♥ 853
♦ A943	♦ 2
♣ K52	♣ AQ74

Contract: 4♠
Opening Lead: ♥Ace

Declarer wins the fourth trick and sees the futility of trying to ruff a Club in dummy. So he embarks on a plan of gaining extra trump tricks by ruffing in hand – normally trumping in dummy is the way to achieve this goal. Declarer ruffs three Diamonds in hand (high of course), each time entering dummy with a trump. On dummy's last trump, a Club is discarded and A/K/Q of Clubs take the last three tricks.

A path with no obstacles probably leads nowhere.

12. **How about a cross-ruff?**

This topic could just as easily been addressed in 'Look Out'. Before embarking on a cross-ruff take all your side suit winners first. Trying to cash them later usually results in them being trumped. Look at the following hand and project what a defender might do while you are merrily cross-ruffing the hand.

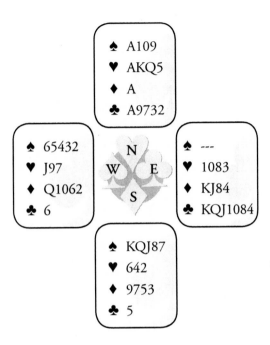

♠ A109
♥ AKQ5
♦ A
♣ A9732

♠ 65432
♥ J97
♦ Q1062
♣ 6

N
W E
S

♠ ---
♥ 1083
♦ KJ84
♣ KQJ1084

♠ KQJ87
♥ 642
♦ 9753
♣ 5

Contract: 6♠   Opening Lead: 6♣

By cross-ruffing, Declarer's 12 tricks consist of the three outside Aces, the ♥King, three Diamond ruffs in dummy, four Club ruffs in hand and a natural trump trick. And if Declarer's problems are only in the trump suit, following are appropriate questions which Declarer can ask himself. Once again, these questions refer to techniques which were addressed in a previous section but are certainly worth revisiting.

13. **Would a trump coup solve my problem?**
    Since the previous explanation of this coup was rather lengthy, revisiting the preparatory steps needed to execute it should suffice.

    (a) Declarer must shorten his trump holding to the same number as held by defender.

    (b) Declarer must cash side suit winners first.

    (c) Declarer must hold a tenace position over said defender.

    (d) Declarer must be leading through said defender at trick 12.

14. Or a 'Coup En Passant'?

One of the constants in the game of Bridge is that there are prerequisites which must be in place when executing a technique, be it a coup or something simpler such as establishing a suit for discards. In the case of this coup, you must be leading through the defender with the higher trump to the hand which has a lower one. And although you don't actually hold a tenace over said defender, the outcome is basically the same. You've made a trump trick out of a card which seemed doomed. Spades are trump. Dummy leads.

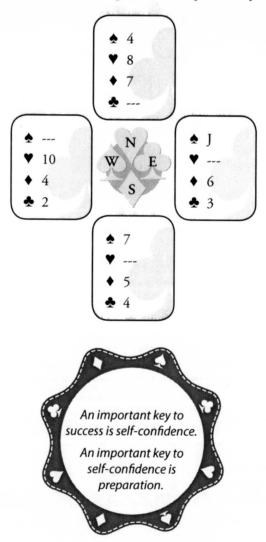

An important key to success is self-confidence.

An important key to self-confidence is preparation.

15. Or a Devil's Coup?

As will be recalled, this is that mysterious card trick which makes a seemingly certain trump trick disappear. The defenders, holding five trump including the Queen and Jack between them would seem to be guaranteed a trump trick. However, careful planning by Declarer and a little luck in distribution of side suits can make that sure trump trick evaporate. Here is the end position which produces this magic. Declarer is on lead, needing all four tricks to fulfill his contract. When he leads the Spade, L.H.O. can ruff high or low or discard a Club. If he ruffs, dummy overruffs and leads a Club. Now R.H.O. is West of the same rock and East of the same hard place. If instead, L.H.O. discards a Club, dummy ruffs low and again leads the Club, producing the same results.

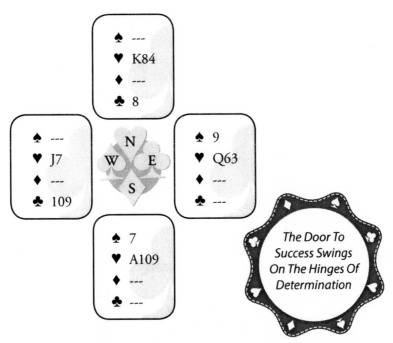

The Door To
Success Swings
On The Hinges Of
Determination

Notice how Declarer holds a tenace position in trump over R.H.O. and dummy has a similar tenace over L.H.O. Not only must the side suits break in such a way as to allow Declarer to cash those winners but Declarer's trump holding can be no more than three. One could almost call this a double trump coup. Declarer is leading through an opponent over whom he has a trump tenace.

The Defenders' Side

The following questions are those which a good defender will be asking as play begins.

1. **Should I begin a passive or active defense?**

   If you suspect a good side suit in dummy, become active even if that means leading or underleading unprotected Aces or Kings. You need to get or develop tricks quickly. Declarer will be discarding losers on that side suit and then trump your winners. If you suspect a short suit in dummy, lead trump. If you suspect a virtually useless dummy adopt a passive mode. Don't give anything away by leading from honours. Top of nothing is a good passive lead. And a trump lead can be passive or active depending on your purpose.

2. **How can I help partner?**

   Helping partner can manifest itself in a number of ways. However, these two should be at the top of the list. Be disciplined in the suit you choose to lead. Once you've settled on which suit to lead as an opening, choose the card within it according to conventional means. This will help partner to begin picturing Declarer's hand. Secondly, if you know what the defence should be, take control and don't give partner a chance to go wrong.

   Here's an example of taking control and not leaving partner to guess a situation or leave him in a position where the obvious lead is not the correct one.

It is a bad plan that admits no modification.

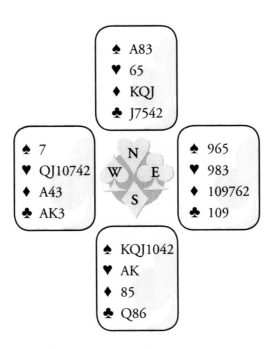

$\spadesuit$ A83
$\heartsuit$ 65
$\diamondsuit$ KQJ
$\clubsuit$ J7542

$\spadesuit$ 7
$\heartsuit$ QJ10742
$\diamondsuit$ A43
$\clubsuit$ AK3

$\spadesuit$ 965
$\heartsuit$ 983
$\diamondsuit$ 109762
$\clubsuit$ 109

$\spadesuit$ KQJ1042
$\heartsuit$ AK
$\diamondsuit$ 85
$\clubsuit$ Q86

Contract: 4$\spadesuit$ Opening Lead: $\clubsuit$Ace

As can be readily seen, the defenders must take the first four tricks or they can simply fold their tents. After L.H.O. cashes two Clubs and gives partner a ruff, partner will certainly lead a Heart (leading up to weakness). This series of plays would hand Declarer the contract. Yet, L.H.O. can defeat the contract by simply cashing the $\diamondsuit$Ace before giving partner his ruff. He who know, goes!

Your discards can also be quite helpful. The following hand is somewhat dramatic but is certainly attention-grabbing.

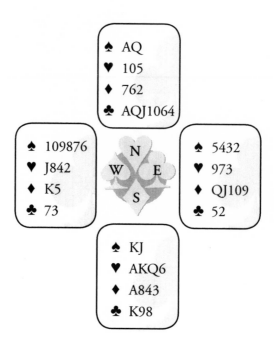

                        ♠ AQ
                        ♥ 105
                        ♦ 762
                        ♣ AQJ1064

    ♠ 109876   N   ♠ 5432
    ♥ J842   W   E   ♥ 973
    ♦ K5   S   ♦ QJ109
    ♣ 73   ♣ 52

                        ♠ KJ
                        ♥ AKQ6
                        ♦ A843
                        ♣ K98

Contract: 7N.T.   Opening Lead: ♠10

Counting winners reveals 12. That's one short and the ideal setting for a squeeze. As Declarer runs the Clubs, West can part with his Spades but is then in dire straits. He must protect the ♦King but is also leery about discarding a Heart from his four card suit. Enter a helpful partner. East simply discards his ♦Queen on the third Club. This tells partner that he has the Diamonds covered. West can then discard his Diamonds and retain his Hearts.

As has just been observed, signals are the legal currency of the defence. They are the way defenders exchange information about their respective hands. However, unless some specifics have been established, they can be misleading or misinterpreted. For example, if you lead an Ace, promising the King, is partner's high spot played to the trick asking for a continuation, giving count or showing suit preference? Although established partnerships have expanded the parameters of the following distinctions, adhering to them during the learning and refinement of each type of signal would be less confusing. Attitude signals are best utilized when partner has led the suit.

Count signals are best given when the lead is from Declarer or dummy.

And suit preference signals should initially be used when giving partner a ruff or dummy is void. Also, extremely important is the card which partner has led. In a previous section, reference was made to the message sent by each card led. Looking back to 'Interpreting The Lead', partner should be able to get a reasonably accurate distribution of the suit from the card led in it. And we won't bother here with one of those ubiquitous leading charts. We've all seen plenty of those.

"Whatta partner..."

3. **Can I neutralize dummy's long suit?**
    Although there are many ways by which this can be accomplished, a classic example is to eliminate an entry to it. This can be accomplished by deliberately sacrificing an honour of your own, as in a Merrimac Coup or by attacking the suit itself before Declarer has taken all your trump.

4. **Will ducking help?**
    If dummy has a strong suit such as KQJ109 and you have the Ace, don't take it when the suit is led. You and partner should be using count signals and partner's carding in the suit will indicate when to take your Ace. Of course, this assumes no other entry to dummy. A low card from partner on the first trick of this suit, indicates an odd number of cards in it. A higher card shows an even number.

5. Can I deceive Declarer without deceiving partner?

Opportunities to deceive Declarer abound. However, partner is often deceived as well and such deception can cause partner to misdefend. A passable way to go about deceptions that have the desired effect is to play deceptively in suits which Declarer attacks not those being attacked by you and partner. Here are a few.

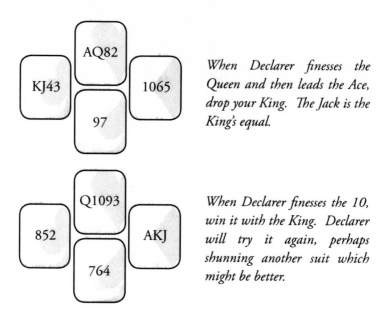

When Declarer finesses the Queen and then leads the Ace, drop your King. The Jack is the King's equal.

When Declarer finesses the 10, win it with the King. Declarer will try it again, perhaps shunning another suit which might be better.

Playing the middle card, in second seat, from holdings such as J109 or J98 will often cause Declarer to miscount the hand.

6. Can I prevent an end play?

Good defenders try to visualize how Declarer is likely to play the hand and then plan their countermeasures. And just as a good Declarer will most certainly begin laying the groundwork for an end play early in the hand, so must defenders lay the ground work to prevent it. Although most players will play second hand low as a matter of course, playing high in that second seat often prevents partner being end played and thwarts Declarer's plan. Here is a hand to illustrate.

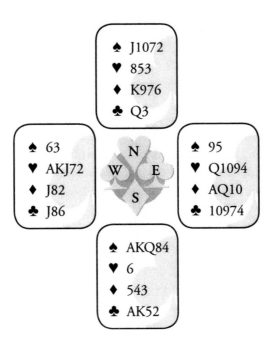

Contract: 4♠   Opening Lead: ♥Ace

With one Heart and possibly three Diamond losers, Declarer realized that an elimination and throw-in was necessary. However, West wasn't asleep as Declarer went about stripping the side suits by drawing trump, ruffing the remaining Heart and clearing the Clubs. When Declarer led a Diamond towards the King, West jumped in with the Jack (second hand high), preventing East from being thrown-in and having to lead up to the King or yield a ruff and sluff. Another method of avoiding being end played is to discard a winner (the potential albatross) and keeping an exit card.

7. **Should I be leading partner's suit?**
    Too many Bridge players, having been indoctrinated with too many myths, adhere to them at all costs. Here are two.

    1) Always lead partner's suit.

    2) Always return partner's suit.

    And the post mortem often reveals that blind obedience to them led to Declarer's success. Although there are good reasons for following such advice, most guidelines in the game have exceptions. And two such exceptions to the leading of partner's suit are when Declarer has shown utter disdain for such a lead by boldly bidding a N.T. game or if the leader has a more demanding lead such as a solid sequence.

As far as returning partner's suit is concerned, here are a couple of contraindications which immediately come to mind. If partner has obviously led top of nothing, there wouldn't appear to be any future in continuing the suit. As well, if dummy now holds a tenace over partner, continuing the suit would again seem foolhardy.

However, if no negative thoughts creep into your mind and you are certain that leading or returning partner's suit is logical, then at least follow the conventional methods. They will maximize the trick taking power of such a suit.

If your opening lead is going to be partner's suit, stop following the archaic policy of leading your highest card. The only time your lead of partner's suit should vary from any other suit is when holding a Doubleton headed by a solitary honour, for example, Kx, Qx, etcetera. Leading the honour in a side suit, hoping to get a ruff, is tantamount to surrender. It will work occasionally and that is all that advocates of such leads remember. However in partner's suit, it is the accepted wisdom as partner will then recognize your holding as a Doubleton. And here are some examples of why the advice of yesteryear doesn't work.

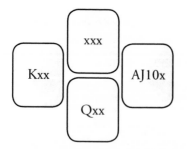

Leading the King has made Declarer's Queen into a winner. Leading third highest, which is normal, doesn't.

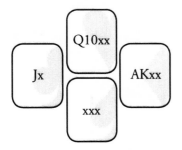

Partner's lead of the Jack announces a Singleton or Doubleton. After cashing the King and Ace, you can give partner a ruff.

When returning partner's suit, here are the accepted guidelines. They help to unblock the suit.

1) With two cards remaining, return the highest.

2) With three cards remaining, return the lowest.

Exceptions to these two guidelines are when you hold two or more intermediates such as the 9, 10 or Jack. In such cases, return the highest intermediate to begin the unblocking process in case partner has more cards in the suit than you do.

Plan the work and work the plan.

8. **Should I play second hand low or third hand high?**
   These twins of advice have survived the test of time, having been left over form Whist, but are also the two guidelines with the most exceptions. As will be seen in the following examples, adhering to them is quite often correct but thinking instead will still win the day.

   First, let's examine why second hand low is good advice and also some exceptions.

1)

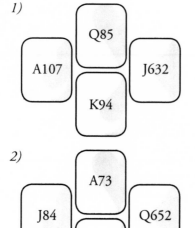

When Declarer leads, you play the 7 and Declarer will only get one trick in the suit. Play the Ace and Declarer gets two.

2)

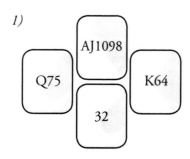

If you play your Jack when Declarer leads the 10, dummy will win with the Ace and by finessing on the second round Declarer will win all three tricks. By playing low on the 10, Declarer will get only two.

And here are some reasons for not following such advice.

1)

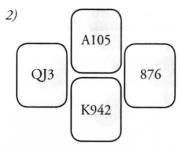

Quite often you can sever communications between Declarer and dummy by playing high in second seat. If there are no other entries to dummy and you suspect that Declarer will finesse twice to produce two entries in this suit, play your Queen when the suit is led the first time.

2)

By splitting your honours in second seat you can prevent Declarer winning a cheap trick. When Declarer leads the two don't play second hand low. If you do, Declarer can win with the 10 and then the Ace and King will win tricks two and three. And if it's a N.T. contract, Declarer will have all four.

3) There are a couple of other reasons for playing high in second seat – to preserve or create an entry to partner's hand, much like the Deschapelles Coup and to prevent partner being end played.

Secondly, let's look at third hand high – why it is good advice and why there are exceptions.

1)

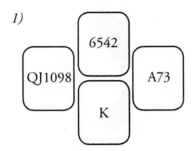

Partner has bid this suit and leads the Queen, denying possession of the King. Percentages say that Declarer has the stiff King. You must play your Ace, third hand high.

2)

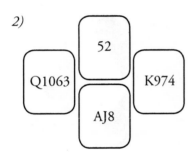

When partner leads the 3, playing your King (third hand high) holds Declarer to one trick. Play any other card in third seat and Declarer wins two tricks and can ruff the third – most undeserved.

Don't play third hand high when:

1) When partner leads the 3, you can't be sure it it's fourth highest from the King, 10 or both. Regardless, play the Jack retaining the Ace over the Queen. If Declarer has the King, it's the only trick he'll get. If he has the 10, he'll likely get no tricks at all.

2) If you have overcalled this suit and partner leads the 7, this is likely the top of a Doubleton. If it is and you have no outside entries, don't play high. Partner will then have one to lead to your runnable suit when he gains the lead in another suit.

9. **Should I split my honours?**

10. Should I cover an honour?

Both of these questions were addressed in the previous section on second hand low and third hand high as well as in numbers four and five in 'Myths'.

11. Is breaking a new suit the correct thing to do?

As referred to in number seven, 'Leading Partner's Suit' is not always advisable. That being the case, breaking a new suit, which is often the wrong approach, should be strongly considered.

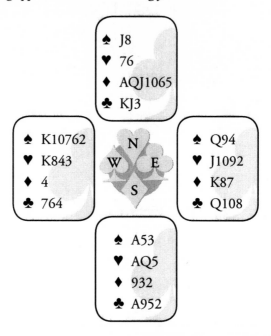

Contract: 3N.T.   Opening Lead: ♠6

Following the 'Rule of 7', Declarer holds up the Ace on the first two rounds – not normally a good idea as a Heart switch would be most unwelcome. However, necessity makes strange bedfellows. After winning the first two Spade tricks, East must realize that continuing Spades would be futile and shift to the ♥Jack. With such a stellar defence, Declarer cannot recover. The ♥Jack lead establishes an entry to West's Spades and as long as East retains the small Heart by unblocking the 10 and 9, the defence will prevail. Defenders must always be projecting how Declarer is likely to play the hand and begin countermeasures.

12. What does the 'Rule of 11' tell me?

Leading charts abound. However, the following is basic.

- *Top of a Sequence*
- *Top of Touching Honours*
- *Third or Fourth Highest*
- *Top of Nothing*
- *Top of a Worthless Doubleton*

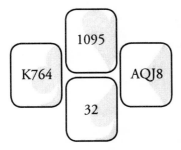

And if the lead is fourth highest, applying the rule allows the leader's partner to begin counting the hand. When the 4 is led, the rule tells leader's partner that Declarer cannot beat the 4 (11 − 4 = 7). All seven cards are visible to East.

And although any card played by East will win the trick, East must begin the unblocking process by winning the lead with a honour and continue the suit by playing an honour. Just in case the leader has a 5 or even 6 card suit, the 8 must be retained as a future lead to partner.

13. Must I avoid giving Declarer a ruff and sluff, or is it safe?

This has always been considered a heinous crime, but in specific situations cannot harm the defence. The detrimental effect of presenting Declarer with a ruff and sluff is that it eliminates a loser for Declarer – a loser he could not have avoided by his own play.

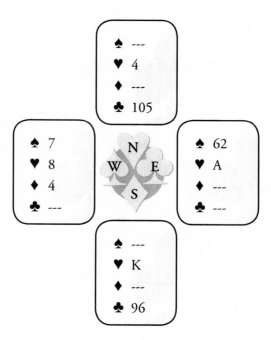

Observe. Clubs are trump with L.H.O. on lead. If a Spade or a Diamond is led, Declarer can discard a Heart from one hand while trumping in the other. In effect, Declarer would win the remaining tricks. If West had led a Heart, Declarer would only win two of the last three. However, if the ♥Ace and King were traded and West had led a Diamond, Declarer would be discarding from a winning suit. No harm done.

14. Can I deceive Declarer?

Opportunities to deceive Declarer abound in this game. However, defender's partner is often deceived as well. Yet the deception might still be worthwhile if it leads to the promised land. The following is a classic.

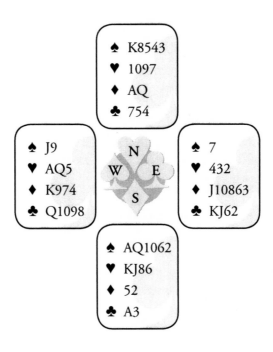

Contract: 4♠   Opening Lead: ♣10

Counting losers, Declarer could lose two ♥, a ♦ and a ♣. A successful finesse in Hearts or Diamonds would eliminate a loser and four Spades would make. However, which finesse? Declarer won the Club lead and put on his thinking cap. Comparing the two alternatives, Declarer correctly tried the Hearts first. He reasoned that if the Heart finesse failed, he still had a fall back position in Diamonds. So he drew two rounds of trump, finishing in dummy. When he ran the Heart 10, West won with the Ace, convincing Declarer to try another Heart finesse instead of the winning one in Diamonds. After all isn't a 100% chance better than 50%. Didn't West's play of the Ace prove that East had the Queen? Chalk up another swindle for a conniving defender.

15. Should I be leading trump?

Although there are as many as 17 very good reasons for attacking their trump on the opening lead, let's simply examine the basic reason. Putting yourself in Declarer's seat, a very sound approach, and envisioning how Declarer might play the hand will seldom lead the defence astray. If Declarer will be trumping losers in dummy, worse still is a cross-ruff, leading trump is a good countermeasure. This would be an attacking mode. Conversely, a trump lead would be passive if it was made because all others were unappealing. The flip side of the coin shows only four where a trump lead would be unwise.

If the reader would like to study this topic more closely, one of this author's previous books, 'The 7 Deadly Sins', covers it more thoroughly.

16. Can I promote a trump trick for our side?

The most common way of accomplishing this task is by means of an uppercut as will be seen in the accompanying hand. And just as techniques such as cross-ruffing, end plays and squeezes (to name but three) require preparation before springing the trap, so it is with trump promotion. It is very often essential that defenders have taken all the winners to which they are entitled before trying for a trump promotion. If they haven't they will be springing the trap prematurely thereby allowing Declarer to discard a loser instead of overtrumping and the defence will have accomplished nothing. And although a trump promotion normally gets the defence just one trump trick, as will be seen in the following hand it can produce two.

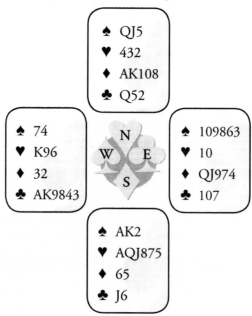

♠ QJ5
♥ 432
♦ AK108
♣ Q52

♠ 74
♥ K96
♦ 32
♣ AK9843

♠ 109863
♥ 10
♦ QJ974
♣ 107

♠ AK2
♥ AQJ875
♦ 65
♣ J6

Once the first two tricks were won by West, he began to look for a fourth trick since his trump King would obviously be the third. Then it occurred to him that he might get a second trump trick if his partner could produce an uppercut with the Jack or 10 of trump. So he led a third Club, knowing that partner and Declarer were void. And as if by magic, partner produced the ♥10 and suddenly, West had his second trump trick. Notice that before the trump promotion was attempted, the defence had taken all that they could in the side suits.

17. **Might we be able to gain control of the trump suit?**

    Most players, when holding an abundance of trump, will make a ruffing lead such as a Singleton or a worthless Doubleton. What these types don't appreciate is that partner will have to gain the lead for such a scenario to materialize. An even worse ruffing lead is Doubleton honour such as Ax, Kx, Qx, etcetera. Aces are meant to capture enemy Kings or Queens and not air. And the King or Queen from these holdings could easily win a trick if Declarer were to try a finesse. These players don't realize that a forcing defence will normally produce more tricks for the defence than will a ruffing defence. Occasionally one of these ruffing leads will prove successful but in the majority of cases are a losing strategy. Just like a compulsive gambler who remembers only the good days, those who make ruffing leads when holding a goodly number of trump, will lose out in the end. Now, back to the forcing defence. The following hand is a good example of this technique. It will also serve as a definition of a forcing defence, a term with which many players are unfamiliar.

♪
What A Difference
A Lead Makes

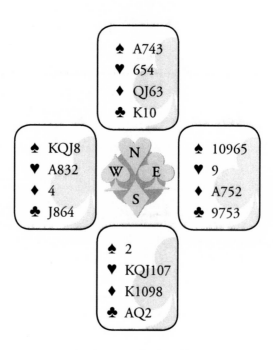

Contract: 4♥   Opening Lead: ?

With a ruffing lead (the Diamond) Declarer cruises home with ten tricks. With a forcing lead (forcing a Declarer to ruff in hand) Declarer can take only nine. The unmistakable value of a forcing defence led to the acronym TLLL – Trump Length, Lead Length, the length being your own good suit.

Neither of these self-questioning lists is complete, but is certainly a sufficient enough number to make a better Declarer or defender of someone who at least asks them. And in the case of defenders, these questions should be going through their minds while Declarer is doing his planning. Too many defenders don't begin to do their thinking until it is their turn to play to a trick. This often gives Declarer valuable information about the location of important cards, resulting in a virtual road map to success.

2) COUNTING

If there was only one word to describe the difference between an expert and the average Bridge player it would be *'Counting'*. Although counting isn't really all that difficult many believe it to be.

Counting Can Even Give A Bottle Of Advil A Headache

After all we count our cards as we begin play. We count points in evaluating our hands for bidding purposes. We count trump during play and apply the *'Rule of 11'* to opening leads. This is really counting. So it is really a natural progression to continue the counting process.

Here are some examples of how simple it can be as well as how the effort put into counting can be utilized.

1. If a player has bid two suits, as Declarer you should know that he will likely be short in trump. So if you are missing four trump including the King, it's very likely his partner has it and probably two others.

2. If your R.H.O. has opened and you are the Declarer, you can count your points, add them to dummy's, assign 13 to R.H.O. and quite accurately conclude how many are in the hand of L.H.O.

To Begin Is To Be Half Done

3. When L.H.O. opens and this bid is followed by two passes, you can bet that your partner's hand is better than that of R.H.O.

4. The *'Rule of 11'* can give you a pretty accurate picture of that suit's distribution. You can have a fairly good idea of the trump distribution by having listened to the bidding. This in turn, will enable you to judge partner's trump holding. Once you have these two suits counted, the other two are then easier to visualize.

5. When a player makes a take-out double, he very likely has at least four cards in one or both major suits if the doubled suit was a minor. If a major, the doubler has four cards in the other major and at least three cards in each minor. The take-out double is basically a three-suited bid showing at least three cards in each of the other three suits.

6. A two-suited overcall like Ghestem, Michael's or the Unusual N.T. is very revealing of the bidder's distribution. Calculating the other distribution becomes that much easier.

7. Watch signals closely. They often reveal the distribution of the suit being led.

8. If you open and R.H.O. fails to balance after two passes, that is likely the hand which holds most of your missing trump.

9. The same logic prevails if R.H.O. fails to respond to his partner's *'Take-Out Double'.*

10. Missing cards in a suit will usually divide as evenly as possible if it is an odd number missing and unevenly if the missing cards are even in number.

11. Pre-emptive bids in a suit are an excellent guide to that suit's distribution around the table.

12. Bids that are obviously higher than H.C.P. would warrant most certainly disclose a distribution hand.

13. Opponents often give count signals when Declarer leads form dummy or his own hand. The suit in which count is given will

frequently begin the countdown of other suits.

14. If L.H.O. is leading partner's suit, the distribution of that suit is often an open book.

15. The second play to a suit by opening leader or third hand will almost always confirm distribution around the table.

16. If the opening lead is in a suit bid by dummy or Declarer, it is likely a Singleton.

17. Try to visualize the distribution of the other three hands during the bidding. This is the beginning of counting.

18. The first discard is very often from a five card suit. The following hands will show the counting of H.C.P., counting winners and/ or losers, as well as the counting of distribution. All of this counting will be addressed from both sides – declaring and defending. First, let's look at Declarer counting tricks, thereby laying the groundwork for success.

Perseverance Is The Father Of Success

Declarer Counting Tricks

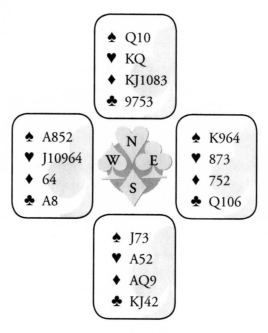

♠ Q10
♥ KQ
♦ KJ1083
♣ 9753

♠ A852
♥ J10964
♦ 64
♣ A8

♠ K964
♥ 873
♦ 752
♣ Q106

♠ J73
♥ A52
♦ AQ9
♣ KJ42

Contract: 3N.T.   Opening Lead: ♥J

With eight top tricks, Declarer's only decision is whether to try for the ninth by attacking the Clubs or Spades. By projecting each line of play it becomes obvious that going after the Spades will result in a ninth trick before the defenders collect five, while trying Clubs might not.

In the second of the two hands showing Declarer putting counting to good use, attacking the longer suit which is normally good technique does not lead to success. Co-incidentally the winning line is again Spades.

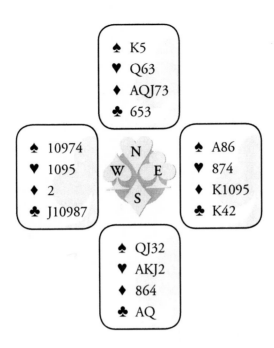

Contract: 3N.T.   Opening Lead: ♣J

With the opening lead producing two Club tricks to go along with the four Hearts and a Diamond Declarer needed only two more to make nine. Once again, projecting two different lines of play will reveal that one leads to success and the other to failure. Taking the Diamond finesse, which is the line too many players would try, would only gain one trick if the suit didn't break favourably. But by counting tricks, Declarer will see that trying Spades will produce two additional tricks and nine in total. Once again, counting wins the day.

In the following hand, a defender finds success by counting.

Defender Counting Tricks

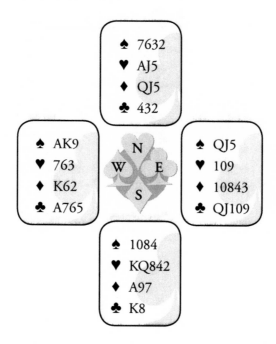

And here is the hand where a defender, by counting Declarer's tricks, is able to come up with the best defence. After an opening of one Heart by South and a raise to two by North ends the auction, West leads the ♠Ace. With partner having the Ace and King of Spades, East realizes that Declarer's points must be in the other three suits. Yet, he was willing to stop at a part score, so his opening hand must be rather mediocre. Having reasoned that much, East embarked on a defence which would maximize defenders' tricks. He dropped the Queen under partner's opening lead. This suggested that the Queen was Singleton or that he also held the Jack. Either way an underlead of the ♠King on trick two would enable East to switch to a minor suit on trick three and conceivably trap Declarer's surmised scant holding. So, on trick two West led the ♠9, East won the Jack and switched to the ♣Queen. After West took the King with the Ace, he cashed a third Spade trick, a fifth trick for the defence and led a Club to partner. This was a tidy six tricks for the defence – tricks which would never have materialized for dogmatic defenders.

Now to the counting of distribution, first by Declarer and then by a defender.

Declarer Counting Distribution

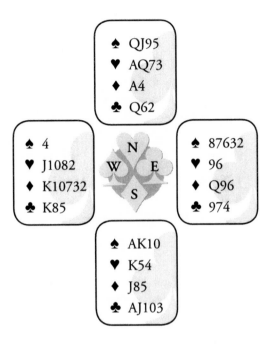

Contract: 4N.T.   Opening Lead: ♦3

After a 1N.T. opening by South and a quantitative raise to 4N.T., an invitation which is declined by South, West leads the fourth highest Diamond. Counting winners, South comes to nine. Trying to get a count on the distribution, Declarer wins the second Diamond and cashes four Spades and three Hearts. With East only following to two Hearts, West is known to have started with precisely four. When West follows to only one Spade trick, his distribution in Spades and Hearts is known (1 and 4). Having led the ♦3 on the opening lead and with the two not yet having shown itself, West would seem to have started with five of those, leaving him with three Clubs. Having to make three discards on the Spade leads, West is left with the master Heart, master Diamond and the protected ♣King. Knowing all this about West's distribution, all Declarer has to do on trick ten is to lead a red card and await his reward for counting. The defence has their opening Diamond trick and the only others will be the ♥Jack and ♦King.

Eddie Kantar says, "Count your winners and then count your losers. If the answer isn't 13, count your cards."

Defender Counting Distribution

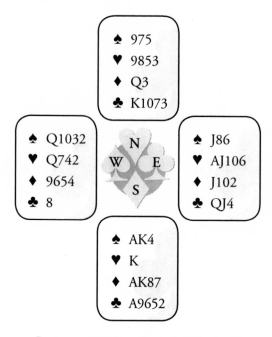

♠ 975
♥ 9853
♦ Q3
♣ K1073

♠ Q1032
♥ Q742
♦ 9654
♣ 8

N
W E
S

♠ J86
♥ AJ106
♦ J102
♣ QJ4

♠ AK4
♥ K
♦ AK87
♣ A9652

Contract: 3N.T.   Opening Lead: ♠2

This hand, from a defender's viewpoint, combines counting with a little deductive reasoning. Declarer felt quite confident after seeing the dummy. The defenders, being good chaps, had not attacked Hearts and if Clubs were to break 2/2 which is to be expected, he had ten easy tricks. However, someone held up the Brink's truck on the way to the bank. After Declarer won the opening lead, he led Ace and another Club. When West showed out, that plan was effectively scuttled. After East won the third Club, he put on his thinking cap. West had obviously led his fourth highest Spade and had shown up with a Singleton Club. He surely would have led from a five card suit rather than from a four bagger had he had one. West's distribution was most certainly 4 – 4 – 4 – 1. That being the case, Declarer had a Singleton Heart. East therefore concluded that, in addition to the Club trick already won, the defence would collect four Hearts for a one trick set. However, just in case Declarer's Singleton was the King, East played the Ace and was justly rewarded for a thoughtful defence.

In the counting of H.C.P., two rules come to mind immediately. The *'Rule of 14'* is a valuable tool when making your opening lead against a 3N.T.

contract. You know Declarer has 16, dummy from 10 to 14 and you can see your own. This will quite accurately indicate how many are held by partner and very often lead you to the best defence.

The *'Rule of 40'* is similar in that it will reveal Declarer's values. As a defender, you can see dummy and your own hand. Having listened to the bidding, you will know whether Declarer has a minimum opening, one of intermediate strength or a strong opener. And of course if the opening bid had been N.T. the picture is even clearer. Following are a couple of hands which will illustrate how informative the counting of points can be.

Defender Counting H.C.P.

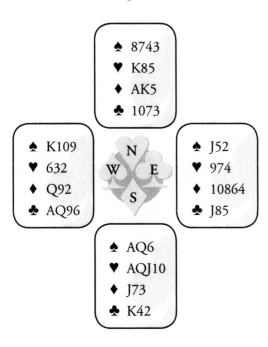

It should be quite obvious to West, on an auction of 1N.T. – 3N.T., that partner is broke. In such cases, adopting a passive defence is called for. And the top of nothing in Hearts certainly fits the bill. Left to his own devices, Declarer has four Heart tricks, one Spade and two Diamonds. If West leads anything but a Heart, Declarer has an eighth trick and with the Spades breaking favourably the ninth trick would likely develop there.

Declarer Counting H.C.P.

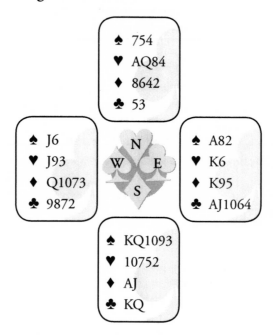

After a 1N.T. opening by east, South becomes Declarer at three Spades. Since South can count 21 points in his hand and dummy there can only be three or four points for West. Declarer takes the Diamond opening lead with his Ace and leads a high Spade. East wins and gives West his Diamond. West has now shown up with two points and when Declarer cashes his trump winner, West plays the Jack. That's three points for West. If East's N.T. opening was 15 to 17, then West cannot have anymore than the Jack of Clubs or Jack of Hearts. Therefore, East most assuredly has the ♥King and Declarer's only hope is that it is Doubleton. Armed with these figures, Declarer cashes the ♥Ace and leads a low Heart. As a result of having counted points, Declarer's only losers are one trick in each suit. Without these calculations, Declarer might have tried the Heart finesse and gone one down.

Before leaving counting, let's examine the important roles played by inference and discovery in the counting process. The following hand illustrates both.

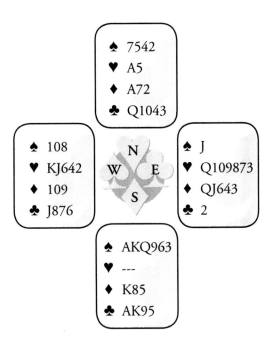

Spades 7542
Hearts A5
Diamonds A72
Clubs Q1043

Spades 108
Hearts KJ642
Diamonds 109
Clubs J876

N
W E
S

Spades J
Hearts Q109873
Diamonds QJ643
Clubs 2

Spades AKQ963
Hearts ---
Diamonds K85
Clubs AK95

Contract: 7♠   Opening Lead: ♠8

Counting losers reveals one Diamond and possibly a Club if the suit splits unfavourably and Declarer plays carelessly. The Diamond loser can be discarded on the ♥Ace. That leaves the Club suit as Declarer's only concern. And it looks like they shouldn't even be a concern. However, as all good Declarers are, do ask, "What can go wrong?"

In this case, Declarer must be ready for a 4/1 split in Clubs. Although five missing cards will normally split 3/2, Declarer must be ready for a 4/1. Declarer should discard a Diamond on the ♥Ace after drawing two rounds of trump. This tells him that West started with a Doubleton Spade. When he clears the Diamond suit, West discards on the third round. This tells Declarer that West started with a Doubleton Diamond as well. These steps were the discovery part of the plan. The inference of the plan is calculating the number of Clubs. Since West had only four pointed cards he had to have nine Hearts and Clubs (the rounded suits). Therefore, he had more room in his hand for Clubs than did his partner. Accordingly, Declarer cashed the Ace and King of Clubs and finessed for the Jack when East showed out on the second Club trick.

3) Courage

According to Webster, courage is 'the capacity to meet danger without giving way to fear.' In the game of Bridge, you might show courage in making a bid which might be fearfully shunned by others. Courage might also manifest itself when making a play that seems suicidal to others but is eminently correct under the circumstances. In #9 of *'Look Out'* a defender leads a King – a play which most would shun – as the only hope of success. That was courageous.

Courage Is Doing
What You Are
Afraid To Do

"Can I be your
partner?"

Following is a hand in which courage is on display during the bidding.

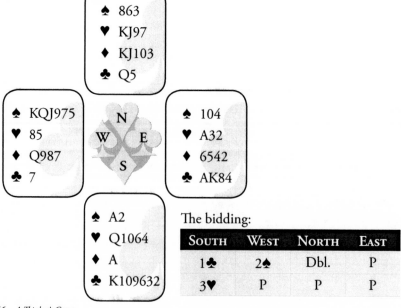

	♠	863
	♥	KJ97
	♦	KJ103
	♣	Q5

♠ KQJ975		♠ 104
♥ 85		♥ A32
♦ Q987		♦ 6542
♣ 7		♣ AK84

	♠	A2
	♥	Q1064
	♦	A
	♣	K109632

The bidding:

South	West	North	East
1♣	2♠	Dbl.	P
3♥	P	P	P

The play in this hand is of no consequence. Declarer can make 3 or 4 Hearts depending on how defenders function. The point of illustrating this hand was to demonstrate the courage shown by North in employing a negative double. A couple of quotes come to mind. As Jerry Helms likes to say, "Find a reason to bid instead of an excuse to pass." "More points are lost by cautious passes than by aggressive bids." – Phillip Alder. It's a bidder's game, get in there. However, there's always the other side of the coin as illustrated by the following story. Playing in a local game, my L.H.O. bid four of their agreed major while uttering, "Oh well, the Lord hates a coward!" To which my partner replied, as he doubled, "Nor is he enamoured with fools."

Being courageous in Bridge manifests itself in a number of ways; during the bidding, in Declarer's play and how defenders conduct themselves in difficult situations.

Bidding

Practically every one of the following examples requires the courage to make bids which are contrary to the teachings of yesteryear. However, it is breaking these ties to stone Ace Bridge which will improve one's game by leaps and bounds. Here they are in no particular order.

1. **Balancing**

   This is a concept which those who are married to H.C.P. and other principles of Bridge's dark ages cannot bring themselves to do. In other words, they lack courage. Although there is much more to balancing than the basics which are about to be illustrated, we are dealing here with courage of implementation and not the specifics. Balancing or protecting – you are really protecting partner – is simply not allowing the bidding to die at a low level when you are in the pass-out seat.

There Is No Defeat
Except From Within

Auctions such as the following are all too common when newer players or those adhering to age-old advice sit in that fourth seat.

1♥ P – P – P

1♦ – P – 2♦ – P
P – P

1♦ – P – 1♠ – P
2♠ – P – P – P

When you are in that pass-out seat, you can be reasonably certain that partner has some values which he was unable to articulate. In the auctions shown, your side probably has as many points as theirs. Examination of all hands in auctions such as these will show that if the opponents have a fit you also have one, in all likelihood. And if their bidding shows that their hands would appear to be misfitted yours will be too.

1♦ – P – 1♠ – P
2♣ – P – 2♥ – P
P – ?

In this case, don't balance. Let them struggle with the misfit. To make this concept more palatable to the uninitiated, simply pretend that you have three more points than you actually do in that fourth seat. Making a bid will then be less traumatizing.

Trusting Yourself To Test The Limits, Is Truly Courage

However, partner must take your re-evaluation into effect, when contemplating a response to your balancing bid, by devaluing his hand by those same three points. Remember these two caveats about balancing – let them play the misfits and devalue your hand by three points if partner has balanced. And when you balance, it will be music to your ears to hear partner say, as the dummy is tabled, "You sure hit pay dirt with your choice of suits, partner!"

*Keep Your
Courage Up And
Conversely It Will
Keep You Up*

♠ K3	♠ Q8743	♠ A103
♥ A109	♥ 92	♥ A984
♦ K542	♦ AK52	♦ QJ72
♣ QJ106	♣ 63	♣ 53

These are hands with which you wouldn't overcall in direct seat (that's the seat when R.H.O. opens) but must bid in the balancing seat. In each case your L.H.O. has opened one Club and this has been passed around to you. With the first hand, bid 1N.T. Remember you have three pretend points. With the second, although you would never bid such a raggedy suit in direct seat, you must show courage and bid one Spade. And with the third, make a take-out double. Don't forget about those three points.

2. **Doubling Part Scores**

Too often, opponent's low level bids which have either stretched the limits or are made in the hope of pushing you higher are passed out and they are left with a net gain on the hand. In cases such as these, they must be punished – double. Occasionally, those doubled bids will make but as Mike Lawrence likes to say, "If your opponents never make a doubled contract, you aren't doubling enough." If you have doubts about making such a double, use the Rule of 6 & 4. The rule simply states that, in a competitive auction, if the level to which they bid is added to the number of trump in your hand and the answer is six or higher – double. The second number in the rule refers to the level of their bid and the number of sure trump tricks in your hand. If that total is four or more, once again you should be doubling.

Each of the following hands are in competitive auctions, you side appears to have the balance of power and in each case your hand passes the test for the *'Rule of 6 & 4'*.

♠ J53	In this first hand, after you have raised partner's opening Spade bid to two, they continue to three Hearts. Double!
♥ KJ42	
♦ QJ73	3 + 4 = 7
♣ 65	

♠ KQ4	Here, you open one Heart. Partner raises and R.H.O. gets to three Spades. Double!
♥ KJ762	3 + 3 = 6 and 3 + 2 *(sure trump tricks)* = 5
♦ A8	
♣ J104	

♠ KJ53	In this hand, you reach two Diamonds with no response from partner. Your R.H.O. bids to two Spades. Double!
♥ 9	
♦ AK1096	2 + 4 = 6 and 2 + 2 *(sure trump tricks)* = 4
♣ AJ3	

♠ KQ52	In this last hand, R.H.O. opens one Diamond and you make a take-out double. After they are pushed to three Spades, double! 3 + 4 = 7
♥ KJ74	
♦ 86	
♣ A95	

Don't shrink from these situations Courage!

3. **Passing Partner's Take-Out Double**

   These doubles have been part of the game since before Goren's time. And the prevailing wisdom, until the modern game, was that you were compelled to respond with your best suit. Passing was punishable by stoning. Yet, today's accepted wisdom is that this double can be passed with no suit to bid in response and a minimum of five cards in the doubled suit. However, another bit of wisdom regarding such a pass should be pointed out. The hand making the take-out double has values in the side suits. Declarer and/or dummy will be trumping these valuable assets. As a result of this analysis, the opening leader is commanded to lead trump. This is in an effort to begin the process of cutting down on those ruffs. Failing to do so is also punishable by stoning.

Risk Nothing, Achieve Nothing.

Lose Nothing, Gain Nothing.

Do Nothing, Get Nothing

Look at these hands.

♠ A10643
♥ KJ
♦ 985
♣ 1072

L.H.O.	PART.	R.H.O.	YOU
1♠	Dbl.	P	?

What in the world could you possibly bid with this collection? Better to pass and let L.H.O. struggle. Opener's partner hasn't bid, so it's a good bet that partner is sitting behind opener's side suit values.

♠ 98	**R.H.O.**	**You**	**L.H.O.**	**Part.**
♥ KJ63				
♦ AQ54	1♠	Dbl.	P	P
♣ KJ2				

It sure looks like your L.H.O. has only a Singleton trump. Partner has left in your take-out double. He likely has a hand like yours in the previous example. In both cases the opening lead should be a trump.

The next examples of courageous bidding, although they are not the only ones remaining, will close out this section.

4. **Opening N.T. in the Modern Game**
   Remember the strict requirements for opening N.T. in the past:

   - Only balanced distributions were opened N.T., i.e. 4 – 4 – 3 – 2, 4 – 3 – 3 – 3, 5 – 3 – 3 – 2. And of course the five card suit could never be a major.

   - You never open N.T. with more than one Doubleton.

   - And a six card suit could never be part of a N.T. opener.

A good guideline in situations where you have a N.T. count but not the classic distribution is to open N.T. if you have no convenient rebid. These hands would never have been opened 1N.T. in the old days. The opener would have opened in a suit and, when partner responded, then could have been seen in genuine distress as he searched for the appropriate rebid.

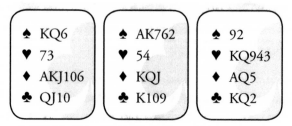

♠ KQ6	♠ AK762	♠ 92
♥ 73	♥ 54	♥ KQ943
♦ AKJ106	♦ KQJ	♦ AQ5
♣ QJ10	♣ K109	♣ KQ2

♠ Q5
♥ QJ
♦ QJ10
♣ AKQ542

♠ QJ10
♥ A5432
♦ KQ
♣ KJ3

♠ 97532
♥ AQ3
♦ KJ2
♣ KQ

Wouldn't a N.T. opening have made partner's response and your rebid much easier. Of course you must be thick-skinned as well as courageous to have opened 1N.T. with each of these hands. And if you do open each of these hands 1N.T. watch out for the purists. They might even call the Bridge police.

(a) Stayman

In days of yore, responding 2 Clubs (Stayman) with less than eight points was considered a crime against humanity. Yet, today these hands are automatic Stayman responses with a pass after opener responds.

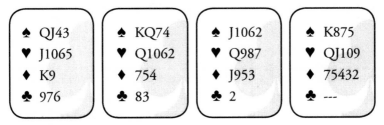

(b) Transfers

When transferring, liberties such as those taken in responding with Stayman are much easier to accept. Here are some hands to illustrate.

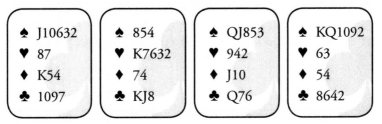

With hands such as these, passing after partner accepts the transfer is the prevailing wisdom. With stronger hands you could invite game by bidding three of the major (you should have six cards) or 2N.T. If you feel game is certain, bid it – either 3N.T. or four of the major. Bidding 3N.T. gives partner a choice.

(c) Responding With A Long Minor
Once again, display some courage, bid 3N.T. if your count warrants a game try. If your hand contains the same long minor but lacks game-going values, a transfer to the minor would be in order.

Defence
When considering the courage required to make seemingly suicidal yet eminently sound plays, defensive coups such as Merrimac and Deschapelles immediately come to mind. Both were explained fully in the section on Coups but are being mentioned here as prime examples of the courage needed to defeat supposedly ironclad contracts. Briefly the Merrimac Coup deliberately sacrifices a King which would have been a certain trick, in an effort to cut communication between Declarer and dummy. In the Deschapelle, a similar sacrifice creates an entry to partner's hand.

Here are two hands to illustrate each of these courageous plays.

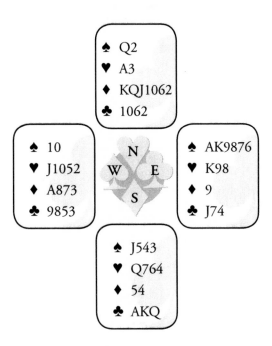

Contract: 3 N.T.   Opening Lead: ♠10

The ♠10 was a natural lead since East had overcalled in that suit. It was obvious to East that Declarer would need the Diamonds to fulfill his contract. East also realized that if Declarer had the Ace and another Diamond, the Diamond suit could not be neutralized. However, if the ♥Ace was the only entry to dummy, it had to be removed before the Diamonds were established. So upon winning the opening lead, East put down his ♥King. End of story.

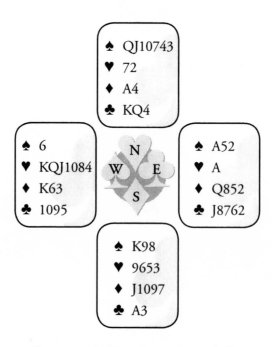

Contract: 3N.T.   Opening Lead: ♥K

Unfortunately, East did not have a Heart to lead back to partner. However, by a process of elimination, East was able to find another way to partner's hand. If that entry were in Spades or Clubs, there would be no problem. But if West's only entry was in Diamonds, immediate action was necessary. With these thoughts completed, East led his ♦Queen in an effort to establish partner's hoped-for ♦King as an entry to his Hearts. The previous hand was the Merrimac Coup. This one is the Deschapelle. It should be noted that there was an inference made by east. This is one of those necessary projections which was referred to in 'Counting'.

Another courageous play which defender might employ is an overtake. As it applies to defenders, it follows the principle of taking control when you have a better idea, than partner, of the defence required.

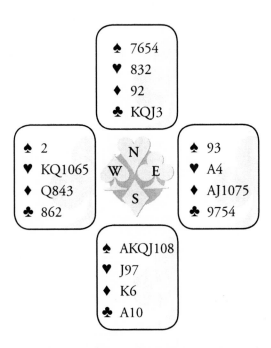

Contract: 4♠   Opening Lead: ♥K

From East's viewpoint, two Heart tricks, a Heart ruff and one Diamond would be a one trick set. The two Heart tricks were obvious because leading the ♥King promised the Queen. Therefore East overtook partner's opening lead and before leading back a second Heart, cashed the ♦Ace to simplify matters for partner. As matters unfolded the defence didn't need the Heart ruff, taking three Hearts instead.

Here is another defensive overtake.

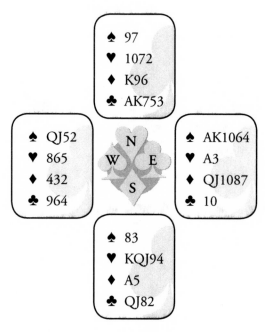

Contract: 4♥   Opening Lead: ♠Q

This is one of those contracts which is often made without defenders even being aware that they could have defeated it. This can be accomplished by the simple expedient of overtaking the opening lead. If East is counting tricks, he can see two Spades, a Club ruff and the trump Ace. It is a very simple matter to overtake the ♠Queen, lead the Singleton Club and await your reward for such brilliance. When Declarer leads trump, take your Ace and lead to partner's ♠Jack and it shouldn't take partner long to realize that you had played the hand this way because you had a Singleton Club and wanted a ruff. But if partner started with five Spades your cause was hopeless.

Declaring

There are many ways in which Declarer can demonstrate courage during the play. Here are some of them.

1. Side suit winners

2. Sacrificing a trick

3. Sacrificing an honour

4. Ducking

5. Last trump as entry

6. Trump blocking

7. Unnecessary finesse

8. Winning with high card

9. Discarding the blocking card

It should be noted that the sample hands which follow are not so much examples of the winning techniques which are often the only road to success but, in fact illustrate the courage needed to pursue a line, which others might define as foolish or that these same critics couldn't even envision.

1. **The Cross-Ruff**

   When aspiring Bridge players first see the advantages of cross-ruffing a hand, they can hardly contain their enthusiasm. They are much like finessaholics who see a finesse and seem duty-bound to take it, regardless of the possible outcome. The cross-ruffers eventually learn, the hard way, that first cashing winners in side suits is the only acceptable line of play.

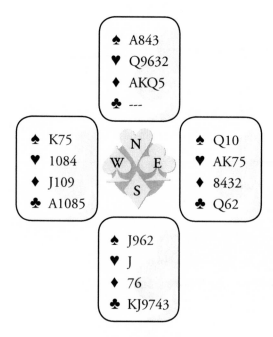

Contract: 4♠   Opening Lead: ♠5

Although counting losers is the norm in suit contracts, it is quite often very revealing to count winners. Also, counting losers in a hand which has so many, as does this one, is far too discouraging. The ten winners in this hand will be the three top Diamonds, a top Spade and three ruffs on each side of the table. However, if Declarer wins trick #1 and concedes a Heart, the defender winning that Heart will quickly lead a second trump and effectively scuttle Declarer's 'Plan A' with no 'Plan B' available. Declarer must display some courage and cash the top Diamonds, pitching a Heart, before embarking on the cross-ruff.

2. **Sacrificing A Trick Or Two**
    A situation which is quite painful to Declarer is not being able to reach the opposite hand when it contains desperately needed winners. There are times when this dilemma is of Declarer's own making but other times when said entry simply does not exist. However, there are also times when a conscientious Declarer can create an entry to the desired hand by careful handling of assets.

Such is the case in the following hand.

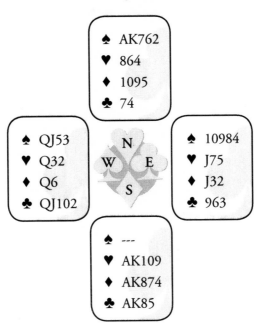

♠ AK762
♥ 864
♦ 1095
♣ 74

♠ QJ53   N   ♠ 10984
♥ Q32 W   E ♥ J75
♦ Q6   S   ♦ J32
♣ QJ102   ♣ 963

♠ ---
♥ AK109
♦ AK874
♣ AK85

Contract: 3N.T.   Opening Lead: ♣Q

If Declarer were to simply cash all the top cards in each suit and
the Q/J of Diamonds were to drop Doubleton, 11 tricks would
be in the bag. Or would they? In case you didn't notice there
is no entry to dummy and those two Spade tricks. Suddenly 11
tricks have become six since the missing Diamond honours are
unlikely to drop Doubleton. However, Declarer can force an
entry to dummy. Don't read any further until you see it. Have
you the courage to win the opening lead and immediately lead a
Diamond towards the dummy?

3. Sacrificing An Honour

Have you the courage to give away one of your top cards, especially
when you are already well short of your goal? Experienced
players display such generosity on a regular basis while newer
players can't quite make themselves show such largesse. And yet,
as the following hand will demonstrate this is exactly what the
doctor ordered if success is to be achieved.

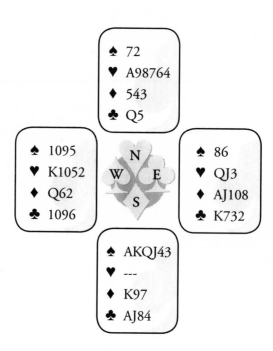

Contract: 4♠   Opening Lead: ♠10

There would appear to be one Club and three Diamond losers. One of the Diamond losers could be discarded on the ♥Ace but dummy has no entry. Enter the resourceful Declarer, stage left. Declarer can win the opening lead, draw the remaining trump and then try to force an entry to dummy by leading the ♣Jack. If R.H.O. wins the King, Declarer can enter dummy with the Queen and discard a Diamond on the ♥Ace, making ten tricks. If R.H.O. opponent refuses the Jack, it becomes Declarer's tenth trick as the Club loser is eliminated. Did you see this play and have the courage to try it?

4. **Ducking**

As has been mentioned, ducking and holding-up are really similar techniques, the difference being that ducking is employed in developing one's own suit while holding-up is utilized in an effort to hinder defenders in developing theirs. Here's a hand where ducking is a necessary Declarer tool.

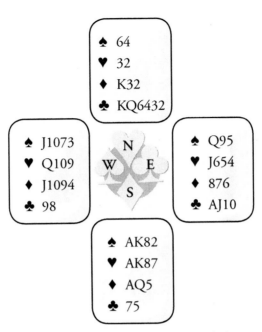

Contract: 3N.T.   Opening Lead: ♦J

There are seven tricks available in the three top ranked suits. Anymore must come from Clubs. However, a clever R.H.O. will refuse the first Club trick and win the second, effectively scuttling Declarer's plan. But look what happens if Declarer does the refusing before R.H.O. After winning trick one in hand, carefully retaining dummy's King as a later entry, Declarer plays a small Club from each hand. When Declarer regains the lead, a second Club is led and R.H.O. must take it, otherwise it becomes Declarer's ninth trick.

5. **Retaining Trump As An Entry**
   There are four basic reasons for delaying the drawing of trump. So that the reader doesn't have to look back in the book, here they are again.

   (a) Declarer can't afford to lose the lead.

   (b) A side suit must be established first.

   (c) Dummy's trump are needed for ruffing.

   (d) Dummy's trump are needed as entries.

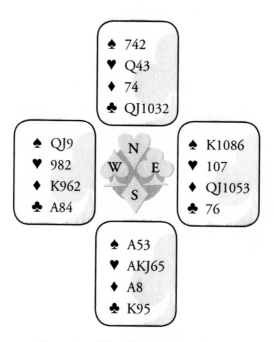

♠ 742
♥ Q43
♦ 74
♣ QJ1032

♠ QJ9
♥ 982
♦ K962
♣ A84

N
W E
S

♠ K1086
♥ 107
♦ QJ1053
♣ 76

♠ A53
♥ AKJ65
♦ A8
♣ K95

Contract: 4♥   Opening Lead: ♠Q

Declarer can discard one of four losers on the dummy's establishable Club suit but how to get to them. A good defender will hold-up the Ace for one round. Holding-up for two would hand Declarer a ninth trick and Declarer wouldn't need to discard a loser on dummy's Clubs. The proper line is to win the first or second Spade and draw two rounds of trump.

This is risky because it might result in a Club rough. However, all is well because a Bridge writer is trying to make a point. Upon losing the Club, Declarer wins any return, draws the last trump by leading to dummy's Queen and discards a Diamond loser on a Club winner. Ah! Such courage.

Knowing What Needs To Be Done But Not Doing It Is a Lack Of Courage On Display

6. Trump Blockage

Lack of transportation between Declarer's and dummy's hands is one of the more difficult problems faced by Declarer during the play. And unblocking is one of the ways in which this dilemma can be resolved. Although most Declarers can understand the need and accept the necessity of doing so in side suits, they have difficulty unblocking in trump – such a waste. Yet this is exactly what Declarer had to do in this hand.

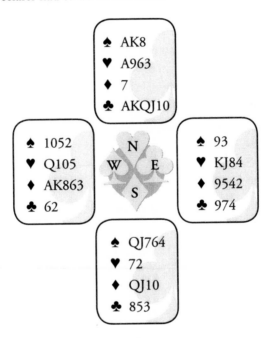

Contract: 6♠   Opening Lead: ♦A

Having responded a Spade to a Club opening, Declarer ended in six. L.H.O. having won the opening trick, began searching for a lead to trick number two. Being from the old school, leading trump would be sacrilege and not wanting to lead a Club, with that powerful suit in dummy or to lead away from the ♥Queen, L.H.O. continued with a Diamond. Declarer was now at that familiar crossroad. If the Diamond was trumped with the 8, there would be no entry to Declarer's hand and the enemy's trump could not be drawn. After a moment in the think tank, Declarer trumped high, cashed the remaining high trump in dummy and led the 8. Thusly, Declarer was able to extract the remaining trump and then discard the remaining Heart and Diamond losers on dummy's Clubs. Perhaps this wasn't as courageous as it was a play *'Born of Necessity'*.

7. **Unnecessary Finesse**

The finessaholic takes a finesse because it's there. Experienced Declarers take a finesse only if it's necessary. And that necessity might be because the extra trick which a successful finesse produces is needed to fulfill a contract or it might be needed to produce another entry. While the unnecessary finesse taken by an addict is called a practice finesse because it gains nothing, the finesse taken by an experienced Declarer has a definite purpose to it. And as pointed out in number three, sacrificing an honour is painful but frequently necessary. As can be seen in the following, a seemingly unnecessary finesse is needed to unblock a suit.

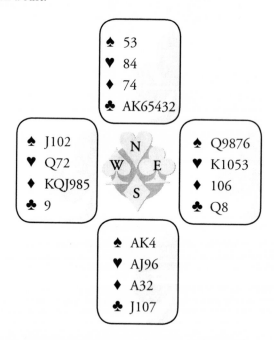

Contract: 3 N.T.   Opening Lead: ♦K

Looking closely at the Club suit reveals that it is blocked. Even if Declarer drops the Jack and 10 under the Ace and King, the 7 will take the third round and all those additional Club tricks in dummy will go for naught. To avoid such a miscarriage of justice, simply lead the Jack and let it ride if L.H.O. doesn't produce the Queen. And if the Queen is played, all is well. It can be taken by the Ace and a Club led back to the 10. The whole suit will now run. If the opening Club lead loses to R.H.O., a trick has been sacrificed for the greater good. Of course Declarer will have waited for the third Diamond before taking the Ace so that R.H.O. will have none to lead after winning the Club.

8. **Unnecessarily High**

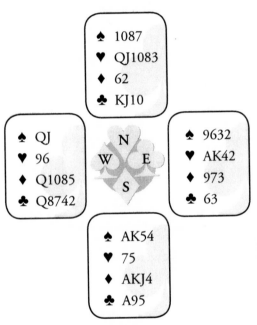

Contract: 3N.T.   Opening Lead: ♣4

Holding four of the five Club honours in the combined hands, Declarer could be quite certain that the opening lead was fourth highest from the Queen. Armed with that knowledge and needing to bring in the Heart suit which would require a second entry to dummy, Declarer won the first trick with the Ace and not the nine. The unplanning Declarer would have won it as cheaply as possible. Having taken this courageous but necessary first step, Declarer proceeded to establish the Hearts and was rewarded with ten tricks.

9. Discarding The Block

It is difficult to discard an honour at any time, especially if it is a winner and particularly for newer players. However, that is precisely what is required in the following hand.

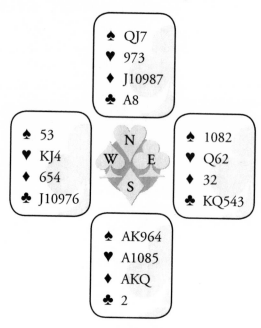

♠ QJ7
♥ 973
♦ J10987
♣ A8

♠ 53
♥ KJ4
♦ 654
♣ J10976

♠ 1082
♥ Q62
♦ 32
♣ KQ543

♠ AK964
♥ A1085
♦ AKQ
♣ 2

Contract: 6♠   Opening Lead: ♣J

At first glance, this hand looks like it has two Heart losers. Even if the Diamonds weren't blocked they would only offer two discards. With the hints given in the previous sentence and the introductory comments, the way to the promised land should be a little clearer. Can you see your way? Don't read any further until you have at least tried.

As is always the case, once the solution has been pointed out, it is so obvious that one wonders why it wasn't obvious immediately.

Painful as it is, you must discard a high Diamond from your hand, but where? There is but one way – win the opening lead and immediately lead dummy's remaining Club, discarding her ladyship. Upon regaining the lead, draw two rounds of trump with the Ace and King. Don't draw a third round since

Dummy's last trump is needed as an entry. At this point, it is reasonably safe to cash the two high Diamonds. When five cards are missing, they normally divide 3/2. And if the split is 4/1 and one of the high Diamonds gets trumped, the hand couldn't have been made anyway. And it's always possible that the defenders with the Diamond shortage doesn't have the remaining trump. Now a trump can be led to dummy and Declarer's three losing Hearts can be discarded on dummy's established Diamonds.

CPSIA information can be obtained at www.ICGtesting.com
Printed in the USA
LVOW06s1407071214

417626LV00004B/268/P